The Role Relationship of Men and Women

New Testament Teaching

The Role Relationship of Men and Women

New Testament Teaching

George W. Knight III

With an essay
"Does *kephalē* ('head') Mean 'Source'
or 'Authority Over' in Greek Literature?
A Survey of 2,336 Examples"
by **Wayne Grudem**

MOODY PRESS
CHICAGO

Previously titled *The New Testament Teaching on the Role Relationship of Men and Women.*

All Scripture quotations, except those noted otherwise, are from the *New American Standard Bible,* ©1960, 1962, 1963, 1968, 1971, 1972, 1973, 1975, and 1977 by The Lockman Foundation and are used by permission.

Appendix 1, "Does *kephalē* ('head') Mean 'Source' or 'Authority Over' in Greek Literature? A Survey of 2,336 Examples" is ©1985 by Wayne Grudem. All Scripture quotations in this appendix are from translations provided by the author of the appendix.

Appendix 2, "Office in the New Testament," is reprinted from *Acts of the Reformed Ecumenical Synod: Australia 1972,* pp. 52–58, by permission of the Reformed Ecumenical Synod.

Revised, 1985

Library of Congress Cataloging in Publication Data

Knight, George W. (George William), 1931–
 The role relationship of men and women.

 Rev. ed. of: The New Testament teaching on the role relationship of men and women. ©1977.
 Includes bibliographical references and index.
 1. Bible. N.T.—Criticism, interpretation, etc.—
Addresses, essays, lectures. 2. Sex role—Biblical
teaching—Addresses, essays, lectures. I. Grudem,
Wayne A. II. Knight, George W. (George William),
1931–   . New Testament teaching on the role
relationship of men and women. III. Title.
BS2545.S37K55   1985   261.8'343   85-4858
ISBN 0-8024-7369-5 (pbk.)

 1 2 3 4 5 6 7 Printing/GB/Year 90 89 88 87 86 85

Printed in the United States of America

Contents

Preface

This book is an attempt to set forth the New Testament teaching concerning the relationship of men and women in the teaching and ruling offices and functions in the church, as well as in marriage and the family. I have chosen to speak of this relationship as a *role relationship* in which the question of authority, headship, or leadership is in view. Rather than attempt a formal definition here, I would refer the reader to the text of the book itself. I do not regard this role relationship as assigned in the drama of life by our culture or society, but as ordained by God for all cultures, societies, and times. This role relationship was established by God in the way He created man and woman in relation to one another, and it continues to manifest itself through the aspect of masculinity and femininity.

It should not be presumed that every relationship between or among men and women is a role relationship in which headship or authority is in question. There are many relationships in which this role question is not involved. That is true also with the people involved in the various other role relationships established in Scripture—parents and children, employers and employees, civil authorities and citizens, elders or church officers and the members of the church. When, for example, employers and employees join in concerted worship, this is not the sphere of employment, and their roles are not then operative. At that moment they enjoy the commonality of the priesthood of believers and the equality of being joint heirs. The same is true in one-on-one personal relationships in which no specific role is in question. That is not to compartmentalize life but to recognize that there are, indeed, appropriate and God-ordained spheres. To look at it from another vantage point, we may say that in role relationships both factors are present simultaneously. For example, the husband is the head of his wife, and at the same time they are equals and joint heirs of the grace of life.

The preceding paragraph is intended simply to introduce a word of caution. Not every relationship that exists between man and woman is that particular role relationship of which the New Testament speaks. In other spheres, men and women are not related as husband and wife or as elders and people, but as those who are mutually dependent upon one another; they relate to one another outside of a particular sphere of authority. Of course, no role assigned by God is completely shed in the psychological and sociological dimensions of our lives. And the apostle urges that the questions of age and sex always be kept in mind, even when the minister authoritatively admonishes the members of his congregation, as we see in 1 Timothy 5:1–2. Even though older men and women are not the actual father and mother of Timothy the minister, he must appeal to them as a father or mother. Likewise he must appeal to younger women as sisters, in all purity. That passage shows that the questions of age and sex may never be completely disregarded, even by the one exercising authority! To return to our caution, not every relationship between men and women is that of the structural and appropriate role relationship, but every relationship does have the overtone of one's maleness or femaleness.

This book focuses on the question of admitting women to the teaching and ruling offices and functions of the church. That is the issue most debated and discussed. It must be clearly kept in mind that the author understands the New Testament to distinguish between those offices and functions and other functions and offices, such as diaconal ones. The question of the marriage relationship will not be dealt with in depth, but only as an introduction and transition to the question of the teaching and ruling offices and functions. Therefore, the section on marriage devoted to a positive exposition is exceedingly brief. Further exposition would have shifted the focus of the book. However, because the basis for the New Testament form of marriage, with its concept of the male head, and for the form of the teaching-ruling offices are the same and interlocked, it is imperative to approach the latter through the former.

Essentially, two strands proceed side by side throughout the book: the first and most important is the exposition of scriptural passages; the second is the answer to objections, particularly to the normativity of scriptural teaching or to the historic exegesis or understanding of scriptural passages.

In substance, the book contains three major essays (much expanded and rearranged) and considerable additional material. The author would express appreciation to all the publications for permission to utilize in rewritten form material that first appeared in their pages. The major part of the exposition of Scripture appeared in the *Journal of the Evangelical Theological Society* 18 (1975). The hermeneutical question of how one should interpret and apply the Scriptures is a major question, and it arises in this book in the first set of objections. If the New Testament speaks about slaves, kings, and women, why do we not treat that material in the same way? The answer to that question of interpretation was originally given in abbreviated form in *The Presbyterian Journal*, 15 September 1976. But there are many more questions about and objections to the historic and traditional exegesis, and the answer to the next set of objections reflects an interaction with Paul K. Jewett, Letha Scanzoni, and Nancy Hardesty that originally appeared in *Christianity Today*, 9 April 1976. Appreciation is extended to the Reformed Ecumenical Synod for permission to reproduce Appendix 2.

I am particularly indebted to and appreciative of the editorial services of Allan Fisher. Mrs. June Dare and Mrs. Robyn Crane, members of the secretarial staff of Covenant Theological Seminary, have done outstanding work in preparing the manuscript for publication.

I offer this book with the prayer that faithfulness to the norm and spirit of God's Word will prevail in the church of Jesus Christ, for the glory of God and the good of all—men and women.

1977

Continued requests for this work while it was out of print have prompted me to issue a revised edition. I am thankful to Moody Press, the new publisher, for making the reissuance and revision possible. This edition contains minor revisions in the text and some bibliographical updating, including a reference to the author's recent article, "AUTHENTEŌ in Reference to Women in I Timothy 2:12." The most important new material is the very valuable excursus on "Does *kephalē* ('head') Mean 'Source' or 'Authority Over' in Greek Literature? A Survey of 2,336 Examples" by Dr. Wayne Grudem, associate professor of New Testament at Trinity Evangelical Divinity School, Deerfield, Illinois. We are all greatly indebted to Dr. Grudem for this research, and I personally am delighted that I may include it as an appendix in this book.

September 1984

1

Introduction

The role relationship of women and men is one of the most discussed topics of our day, in evangelical circles as well as elsewhere. Two books claiming to be written from the evangelical perspective and published in the mid-1970s have aroused considerable interest: *All We're Meant to Be: A Biblical Approach to Women's Liberation,* by Letha Scanzoni and Nancy Hardesty;[1] and *Man as Male and Female: A Study in Sexual Relationships from a Theological Point of View,* by Paul K. Jewett.[2] These authors focus on the necessity for equality in the male-female relationship and presume that that rules out prescribed differences of function in the role relationship. The emphasis on equality and unity reiterated in the great redemptive passage of Galatians 3:28 means, these authors argue, that there is to be no submission of women to men either in the marriage relationship or in the ruling-teaching functions in the church.

I believe that equality and difference of role are not mutually exclusive but are indeed the two sides to the teaching of the

1. Waco, Tex.: Word, 1974.
2. Grand Rapids: Eerdmans, 1975. Followed by his book *The Ordination of Women* (Grand Rapids: Eerdmans, 1980).

Word of God on the subject. It is significant that the apostle Peter joins the two notes of equality and difference of roles in his treatment of the marriage relationship in 1 Peter 3:1–7. While Peter appeals to the husband to honor his wife as a "fellow-heir"—that is, as his equal—he also urges the husband to recognize his wife's femininity (as the "weaker vessel") and the wife to submit to her husband. Likewise, the apostle Paul writes of man and woman as one in Christ (Gal. 3:28), and also of the wife's submission to the headship of her husband (Eph. 5:22ff.; Col. 3:18–19). Equality and role differences are compatible.

That has been the church's understanding of New Testament teaching on the role relationships of citizens and civil authorities, of church members and those who rule over them, of children and parents, even at times of servants and masters, and of wives and husbands. With the exception of servants and masters (which relation the church understood as being regulated by the New Testament but not mandated by God), the church understood those role relationships to be established by God and governed by guidelines given by the Lord and His apostles. Included in those role relationships was that of male and female in marriage, one that evangelicals still recognize as normative.[3] For the same reasons, the church also has upheld a similar relationship between male and female in the ruling-teaching functions in the church; in particular, the passages of 1 Timothy 2:11–15, 1 Corinthians 14:33*b* (or 34)–38, and 1 Corinthians 11:1–16 have been understood as normative in this area.

Not unexpectedly, certain objections have been brought against the uniform New Testament and apostolic teaching. Full, free, and frank discussion of the matter is desirable; it will enable Christians to come to a clearer and more balanced understanding of the total biblical teaching on this subject. But I am distressed that some who have written on the subject seem to abandon the inerrancy of Scripture and the authority of its

3. Cf., for example, Harold Lindsell, *The World, the Flesh, and the Devil* (Washington, D.C.: Canon, 1973), pp. 135–36.

teaching. Even some who claim to be evangelical Christians, who profess submission to the authority of God and His Word, are willing to appeal to the passages in Scripture that seem to support their position and to minimize other passages or declare them to be either wrong or only culturally relative and thus not normative—even when those passages themselves claim to be just the opposite. For example, Jewett, in his most candid and forthright way, says that Paul is wrong in his evaluation of the relationship of man and woman and in his appeal to and understanding of God's creation order in Genesis 1 and 2.[4] He and other evangelicals who hold similar views, when asked whether that is not a denial of the infallibility of the Scriptures, tend to reply—as Jewett did at a conference at Western Theological Seminary (Holland, Michigan)—that they believe in the full inspiration of the Scriptures and in its infallibility in reference to what it intends to teach concerning the area of "faith and life." But the sad and strange outcome of that qualification or limitation of infallibility is that its proponents end up denying what the apostles taught concerning one area of "faith and life." Such a view of infallibility denies even what it purports to save and keep. The unchanging Word becomes the changeable Word that must square with a changing culture, which now has become the norm for man's life.

Others who depart from the church's long-standing view of scriptural teaching on men and women would vigorously object that it is not a matter of one's view of the Bible, but of one's interpretation of the Bible—that is, it is a question of hermeneutics. Virginia R. Mollenkott and others allege that to interpret the Bible as normative in its teachings about man and woman means we must also insist on slavery[5] and government by kings, about both of which the apostles also give instruction. Truly the question of the Bible as God's unchanging Word in man's changing

4. *Man as Male and Female*, pp. 134ff., 139, 145. Cf. also *Theology: News and Notes* (Fuller Seminary), special issue (1976): 20–22.
5. Cf. for example, Mollenkott's foreword in Jewett, *Man as Male and Female*, pp. 11–12.

culture is a question not only of the inspiration and inerrancy of the Bible, but also of the interpretation and application of the Bible to man's changing culture. But a proper interpretation of the Bible, or truly biblical principles of interpretation, will demonstrate that the teachings of the Bible display permanence, continuing relevance, and validity, even in the midst of a changing world and society. Therefore, the very questions raised will aid us in resolving the problem they thrust upon us and upon every thinking man and woman.

The church's traditional understanding of apostolic teaching concerning men and women has been challenged particularly in the area of church life and government. Vigorous discussions in Germany and the Scandinavian countries have led to the majority of Lutherans in particular abandoning the earlier position.[6] Similar studies made in the United States resulted in a predominance of American Lutherans following the Europeans.[7] On a broader plane, most of the older American denominations have also altered their previous positions,[8] and the World Council of Churches has reported that a great number of its member churches have done the same.[9] The Permanent Judicial Commission of one American denomination ruled that an evangelical should not be ordained who said that his understanding of the Scriptures would prohibit him from ordaining a woman to the teaching-ruling office.[10]

6. See the following: Peter Brunner, *The Ministry and the Ministry of Women* (St. Louis: Concordia, 1971); Krister Stendahl, *The Bible and the Role of Women* (Philadelphia: Fortress, 1966); and Fritz Zerbst, *The Office of Woman in the Church* (St. Louis: Concordia, 1955).

7. See the groundwork laid in Raymond Tiemeyer, *The Ordination of Women* (Minneapolis: Augsburg, 1970).

8. For example, the United Methodists, United Church of Christ, Disciples of Christ, etc. For specific statements, see the *Book of Order* of the Presbyterian Church in the U.S.A., chap. VI, sec. 1 and chap. XIV, sec. 1. The *Book of Order* occurs as one of the documents in *The Plan for Reunion* (Prepared by Joint Committee on Presbyterian Union, Final Edition, 1981).

9. Cf., for one example, Brigalia Bam, ed., *What Is Ordination Coming To?* (Geneva: World Council of Churches, 1971).

10. *Minutes of the General Assembly of the United Presbyterian Church in the United States of America, 1975*, pt. 1, pp. 52-54, 254-59. The assembly upheld the Commission, which declared, "It is the responsibility of our Church to deny ordination to one who has refused to ordain women" (p. 258).

That ministerial candidate is not the only evangelical holding to his conviction. The Reformed Ecumenical Synod, when meeting in the Netherlands in 1968 and in Australia in 1972, reaffirmed as the teaching of Scripture the historic Christian understanding of the passages in question.[11] Also, studies coming from the dominant conservative wing of the Lutheran Church—Missouri Synod have reaffirmed the normative character of the passages in 1 Timothy and 1 Corinthians.[12] One might be tempted to generalize that while the more liberal wing of Protestantism has abandoned the historic Christian position, the more conservative wing has reaffirmed it,[13] and that that reflects their respective views of the Bible—its inspiration, inerrancy, and absolute authority. Avowed evangelicals, however, have opted against the historic Christian position. Scanzoni and Hardesty say that Paul's position on the role of women in church life is an expression of the culture of his day and is not normative for ours.[14] Jewett says that Paul's position reflects his rabbinic perspective and is therefore not normative.[15] And a majority of the invited participants in the Thanksgiving Workshop on Evangelical Social Concern voted to seek ordination of women to the teaching-ruling offices of the church, although there was a large dissent[16]

---

11. *Acts of the Reformed Ecumenical Synod: Amsterdam 1968*, p. 35; and *Acts of the Reformed Ecumenical Synod: Australia 1972*, pp. 58f. This last *Acts* includes two extensive reports of the study of Scripture that brought the Synod to that position. See the report of Advisory Committee VI, "Office in the New Testament," presented to the 1972 synod (pp. 52–58). It is included as Appendix 2 to this book.

12. See the last- and first-named books in note 6; also David Scaer, "What Did Saint Paul Want?" *His* 33 (May 1973): 11ff.

13. Two very noteworthy books appeared in the early 1980s: Susan T. Foh, *Women and the Word of God* (Phillipsburg, N.J.: Presbyterian and Reformed, 1980), and James B. Hurley, *Man and Woman in Biblical Perspective* (Grand Rapids: Zondervan, 1981). See also from a non-Protestant perspective the unique work of Stephen B. Clark, *Man and Woman in Christ* (Ann Arbor, Mich.: Servant, 1980).

14. *All We're Meant to Be.*

15. *Man as Male and Female.*

16. See the reports in: *Christianity Today*, 20 December 1974, pp. 28f.; *Christian News*, 16 December 1974, pp. 1f. (a Religious News Service report).

The subject, then, is a live one, even within evangelicalism, and it deserves careful study. What follows is a presentation of the biblical evidence first for submission and headship in marriage, and then for submission and headship in the church, as well as answers to the major objections raised against these arguments. The role relationships of men and women in marriage and in the church are founded on exactly the same principles, and the biblical teaching on those two areas of life must stand or fall together.

2

Submission and Headship[1] *in Marriage*

THE BIBLICAL EVIDENCE

The momentous words of Galatians 3:28 provide us with the framework within which any and all differences or role relationships must be seen and considered: "There is neither Jew nor Greek, there is neither slave nor free man, there is neither male nor female; for you are all one in Christ Jesus." Here the apostle, recognizing the differences between Jew and Greek (cf. 1 Cor. 9:19–21) and male and female, affirms that they are brought into one new being in Christ Jesus so that they are all one. With this word he removes any ethnic, national, racial, social, or sexual characteristic as determinative of one's spiritual standing in Jesus Christ. Faith in Christ and nothing else brings one into spiritual unity with Christ and into equality (cf. 1 Cor. 12) with all who are Christ's. The theological underpinnings of this are the facts that all human beings are made in the image of God (cf. Acts 17:26), and that this image is renewed in the

---

1. See Appendix 1 of this book, by Wayne Grudem, "Does *kephalē* ('head') Mean 'Source' or 'Authority Over' in Greek Literature? A Survey of 2,336 Examples."

image of Jesus Christ (Col. 3:10–11; Rom. 8:29; 2 Cor. 3:18). Thus what is said in Galatians 3:28 is reiterated in Colossians 3:10–11 in relation to image renewal in Christ. We may say, therefore, that Paul faithfully reflects the Old Testament teaching of Genesis 1:27, which is that image quality is equally present in male and female. Thus both by creation and now also by the redemption that renews that created image quality, the unity and equality of male and female are most fundamentally affirmed.

So also the apostle Peter affirms this coequality and unity when he speaks of male and female, husband and wife as joint-heirs (*sunklēronomois*) of the grace of life (1 Pet. 3:7). The aspect of Peter's treatment that is noteworthy for our question is that he affirms this spiritual equality in the midst of a passage speaking of a distinct role relationship of wives and husbands—that is, that wives must be in subjection to their husbands (3:1) and that husbands must give honor to their wives as the "weaker vessel" (*asthenesterōi skeuei*, 3:7). The weaker-vessel terminology would seem to be Peter's way of stating the femininity of the woman, comparing the size and muscle strength of her body to that of a man's body, without intending to derogate the woman.[2] Peter has at once joined equality and difference as the two factors that must guide the role relationship. As we shall see later, Paul sees both equality (image-bearers) and difference (masculinity-femininity) to be equally the result of God's creative activity and order, and therefore, both are germane to the question under consideration. He who can reflect Genesis 1:27 in terms of spiritual equality in Galatians 3:28 (and Col. 3:10–11) can also reflect Genesis 2:18–25 in speaking of wives' being in subjection to their husbands as their heads (Eph. 5:22–33; see especially vv. 22, 23, 31, 33). Both facets of creation come to their rightful expression. Spiritual equality may not be negated by sexual differences, because we are both made and renewed in the image of God (Gal. 3:28; Col. 3:10–11). Nor does our spiritual equality as joint-

2. See Gustav Stahlin, *"Asthenēs,"* in *Theological Dictionary of the New Testament,* ed. Gerhard Kittel and Gerhard Friedrich, trans. and ed. Geoffrey W. Bromiley, 9 vols. (Grand Rapids: Eerdmans, 1964–1974) 1:491.

heirs of life remove our maleness and femaleness and the role relationship which that created difference brings to the relation of man and woman as it exists in marriage (1 Pet, 3:1–7; Eph. 5:22–33).

OBJECTION ANSWERED

"IF THE NEW TESTAMENT REQUIRES WIVES TO SUBMIT TO THEIR HUSBANDS, THEN IT ALSO SANCTIONS SLAVERY AND REQUIRES GOVERNMENT BY KINGS."

Opponents of the normative character of the New Testament teaching on the role relationship of men and women often point out that the apostles not only direct wives to submit to husbands, but also require slaves to submit to masters and citizens to kings. And they add that instructions to wives and to slaves are often given in the very same context. They argue that if we accept Paul's teaching about wives submitting to husbands as universally valid and necessary, we must also accept slavery and government by kings as universally valid and necessary.[3] Paul's teaching about wives, they conclude, must be culturally relative.[4]

We will deal with the three areas of slaves and masters, kings and civil government, and husbands and wives, for several reasons. First, those who have advanced this objection to the traditional interpretation and application of the apostolic teaching concerning wives and husbands deserve a response. Second, these subjects touch upon important areas of life—one's work and freedom, one's civil government, and one's marriage relationship. Those intrinsically merit our consideration. Third, because the apostles devoted considerable space to them, these items were important to the apostles and so are automatically

3. See, for example, Virginia R. Mollenkott, *Women, Men, and the Bible* (Nashville: Abingdon, 1977), pp. 92ff.
4. Paul K. Jewett, *Man as Male and Female* (Grand Rapids: Eerdmans, 1975), pp. 137ff., Letha Scanzoni and Nancy Hardesty, *All We're Meant to Be* (Waco: Word, 1974),pp. 91, 107, 202–5.

important to us. Fourth, this objection to apostolic teaching concerning wives and husbands has ramifications for apostolic teaching concerning children and parents. The household regulations given by the apostles usually begin with the subject of wives and husbands and end with the subject of slaves and masters, but in between is the subject of children and parents. So far, these opponents have been silent about whether the teaching concerning children and parents, like the teaching concerning other household relationships, is to be set aside; but their logic, which would have all items in the list of household regulations stand or fall together, would lead one to do just that. And finally, a proper interpretation of these three subjects, noting the similarities in and differences between the ways in which the Bible handles each, will provide us with specific principles of interpretation that will, in turn, help us properly to understand the Bible and apply it to our lives.

Slaves and masters. Restricting ourselves to the New Testament, we find this subject dealt with directly and specifically in Ephesians 6:5–9; Colossians 3:22–25; 1 Timothy 6:1–2; Titus 2:9–10; 1 Peter 2:18ff.; and Philemon. It is clear that the first four passages instruct slaves to honor, obey, and serve their masters, and that Ephesians instructs masters to treat their slaves with goodness in reciprocity, to "do the same things to them" and "give up threatening" (Eph. 6:9). Both slaves and masters are reminded that they have a Lord and Master in heaven whom they serve even in these activities and roles, and that "there is no partiality with Him" (Eph. 6:9; cf. Col. 3:25). That is the essence of the motivation Paul uses in his instructions to slaves and masters.

Now the question for us and our day is: Does Paul's instruction for slaves and masters mean that the Scriptures regard this relationship as a God-ordained institution to be perpetuated? The answer with which we must respond, because of these very passages, is no. The apostle Paul instructs men in the situation in which they find themselves. There is no implication that he, as the spokesman for God, desires to perpetuate that situation. We draw this conclusion from three considerations.

First, nothing in the passages dealing with slaves and masters indicates that the relationship is ordained by God. Paul does not argue, as he does with parents and children and with husbands and wives, that those are God-ordained roles established by God. He only tells the slaves and masters how they should conduct themselves in the situation in which they find themselves, whether it is the best situation or not. (I think that Paul sowed the seed for the abolishment of the slave relationship in his remarks to Philemon concerning Onesimus; see verses 10, 12, 14, 15–17, and especially 21.)

Second, 1 Corinthians 7:20 demonstrates that Paul's approach to life is to direct men to live as Christians in whatever condition they are, neither ignoring that condition in a sinful world nor ranting against it: "Let each man remain in that condition in which he was called." Paul even applies this principle directly to slaves: "Were you called while a slave? Do not worry about it" (1 Cor. 7:21). The apostle recognizes, however, that the slave might be freed, as is apparent in either interpretation of the rest of verse 21, but is especially clear in this translation: "But if you are able also to become free, rather do that."[5] Verse 21, then, makes it clear that Paul can at the same time instruct slaves in how to conduct themselves *and* recognize that their slavery and the institution itself can indeed come to an end. His principle is first and foremost to instruct men in how to live in the socio-economic situation in which they find themselves. He is not establishing or perpetuating slavery at all, but rather telling slaves how to live in a Christian way. The beauty and power of his approach is that Christianity has something to say to men in that difficult situation, rather than simply saying that their situation is hopeless or that they should riot or adopt some other violent course. It is the Christianity of the God of

5. For an outstanding discussion see S. Scott Bartchy, *Mallon Chrēsai: First-Century Slavery and the Interpretation of 1 Corinthians 7:21*, Society of Biblical Literature Dissertation Series, no. 11 (Missoula, Mont.: The Society of Biblical Literature, 1973).

love and mercy who through His apostles finds men and ministers to them in the situations in which they are living.

Third, Paul's approach to slavery is essentially the same as Moses' approach to divorce. Jesus said, "Because of your hardness of heart, Moses permitted you to divorce your wives; but from the beginning it has not been this way" (Matt. 19:8). In my judgment, Jesus indicated that God, through Moses, regulated divorce because of the hardness of their hearts, not because He wanted them to practice divorce. In like manner, God, through the apostles, regulated slavery.

This discussion has shown that God's Word is true and unchanging. It shows how slaves and masters should relate to one another wherever and whenever slavery exists. And because Paul addresses the question of work through or by means of the more specific situation of slavery, those principles concerning work, stripped of their unique slave-master nuances, are still valid for us today in the similar, albeit also different, employee-employer relationship.

The state and its government. Again restricting ourselves to the New Testament, we find this question most directly dealt with in Romans 13:1-7, 1 Peter 2:13-17, and Titus 3:1-3. The point at issue here is that Peter speaks specifically of a king in 1 Peter 2:13, 17. And, of course, it would seem that the highest government official in view in the Pauline passages is also a king, not to mention our Lord's reference to Caesar.

But when Peter says "Submit yourselves for the Lord's sake . . . to a king as the one in authority, or to governors as sent by him" (1 Pet. 2:13), and "Honor the king" (1 Pet. 2:17), he is clearly enunciating a specific application of a general principle. Verse 13 begins, "Submit yourselves for the Lord's sake to every human institution." The principle is not that there must be kings and governors, but that Christians must submit to the human institution of government in whatever form or shape it may take and whoever the civil authorities may be (cf. Titus 3:1ff.)—so long as this allegiance does not conflict with their absolute allegiance to God.

Paul demonstrates the same abiding principle when he states the truth in general terms, using the general phrase "governing authorities" rather than the word "kings": "Let every person be in subjection to the governing authorities" (Rom. 13:1). This understanding is undergirded when one recognizes that Romans 13:1 concludes with a general statement of principle without reference to kings: "For there is no authority except from God, and those which exist are established by God." The sum of the matter is that civil government is an institution ordained by God. The New Testament reference to kings, or even to governors for that matter, is simply a direct application of the principle to the situation that obtained for the original recipients of Peter's first letter. Here we see that the institution of government is ordained by God for all places and every age, and that the form of that institution is whatever form God's providence allows to exist from place to place and from age to age. Again we see that God's Word is unchanging in the midst of man's changing culture.

The marriage relationship. What is the ground for the husband's headship and the wife's submission? Paul appeals persistently to the way God made man and woman and the way He made them to relate to one another. That is seen indirectly in Paul's quotation of Genesis 2:24 in Ephesians 5:31, and directly in both his appeal to the law in 1 Corinthians 14:34 and his expression of the law's substance in 1 Timothy 2:13–14 ("For it was Adam who was first created, and then Eve"). Paul's exposition of Genesis 2:21–24, found in 1 Corinthians 11:8–9, is: "For man does not originate from woman, but woman from man; for indeed man was not created for the woman's sake, but woman for the man's sake." Paul offers this exposition as the basis for his statement that "the man is the head of a woman."

This argument is based not on some cultural consideration that changes as man's culture changes, but on the most basic of considerations for human conduct–how God created man and woman in relation to one another. Just as Jesus appeals to God's creation activity to indicate God's will for permanence in marriage, so Paul, Christ's apostle, appeals to creation to indicate the relationship that husbands and wives should sustain to each other (cf. Matt. 19:4–6).

Some might suggest that the Bible, as in the case of slavery, does not *institute* marriage but only *regulates* it as an institutional phenomenon that exists in man's culture. Surely the word of our Lord Jesus concerning marriage is adequate refutation of that idea: "What therefore God has joined together, let no man separate" (Matt. 19:6). This is not an item, like the relationship of slaves and masters, that Christ and the apostles regulate but do not desire to continue. On the contrary, Christ desires to continue the very form of marriage.

Others might suggest that this subject of woman and man should be handled as the question of kings was handled. That is, marriage is permanent, but the identity of the head or the authority can change along with man's culture. When in man's culture kings rule, Christian men and women should submit to kings; and when in man's culture the husband rules, wives should submit to husbands. All the Bible wants, they say, to preserve is stability in government and marriage, and it is not concerned with *who* rules in each realm.

The fallacy of that argument is that it overturns the very form that the apostles seek to establish and continue as a permanent element in marriage. The apostles do not argue just for some authority in marriage, but explicitly and particularly for man's authority and headship over woman and woman's submission to man (Eph. 5:22–33; Col. 3:18–19; 1 Pet. 3:1–7). For the basis of man's headship and woman's submission, the apostle Paul appeals to the analogy of God the Father's headship over Jesus Christ, His incarnate Son (1 Cor. 11:3); to God's creative activity (creating woman *from* man) and its significance (1 Cor. 11:8–9; see Gen. 2:18–24); and to the analogy of Christ's headship over the church and its submission to Him (Eph. 5:22–33). With full authority and with absolute and permanent reasons, Paul argues for the form of the relationship between man and woman. One would have to deny Paul's argument or his explanation and application of Genesis 2 to overturn the fact that this is the teaching of the apostles that they intended to be believed and obeyed.

The teaching of the Word of God concerning slaves and masters is true and unchanging for that relationship, even though the Word of God itself recognizes that the relationship may completely pass away; the teaching of the Word of God concerning civil government is true and unchanging even though the Word of God recognizes that the form of civil government—for example, kings—may change; the teaching of the Word of God concerning man and woman in marriage is true and unchanging because that relationship is established by God's creative activity. In this last relationship, Christians must oppose man's changing culture if and when it seeks to revise or overturn the standard of God. Notice carefully that the unchanging Word of God speaks authoritatively to the culture of man that God allows to pass away (slavery), to the culture of man that God allows man to change appropriately (civil government), and to the culture of man that God requires man to maintain (the form of authority and headship in marriage). It is imperative that we distinguish the areas of man's culture and not confuse them, as some have done and are doing. We must always understand, believe, and apply God's unchanging Word in the way in which He directs us from within that Word itself. Only then does it continue to be the authoritative Word of God that stands over man's changing culture.

3

Submission and Headship in the Church

THE BIBLICAL EVIDENCE

When we focus on the question of the role relationship in the teaching-ruling functions in the church, it is appropriate to ask if that question is dealt with explicitly in the New Testament. If it is, we must concentrate our attention on such didactic passages. That is basic to the proper handling of the Scriptures and the resolution of any question, and will prevent us from drawing erroneous conclusions from passages that treat the subject only incidentally. In that case we have three passages: 1 Timothy 2:11–15, which most clearly gives both the apostle Paul's verdict and his reason for that verdict; 1 Corinthians 11:1–16, which explains the significance of that reason; and 1 Corinthians 14:33b–38, which presents the apostle's command and his reason for it in more general terms.

1 TIMOTHY 2:11–15

The setting for 1 Timothy 2:11–15 is a letter in which Paul instructs Timothy about the life of the church. Paul says explicitly that he is writing so that Timothy may "know how one ought to conduct himself in the household of God, which is the church of the living God, the pillar and support of the truth" (3:14–15). While the limits of this reference may extend to the whole letter, it certainly encompasses at least chapters 2 and 3. In chapter 2, Paul first writes about prayer, referring particularly to the responsibility of men. Then he turns to women and speaks of the need for modesty in dress, for a repudiation of ostentatiousness and a concentration instead on the adornment of good works (2:9–10).

After a general statement that requests women to learn in quietness and all subjection (*pasēi hypotagēi; hypotagē,* or subjection, is also the keynote found in the wife-husband relationship [Eph. 5; 1 Pet. 3]), he then makes that aspect of subjection more explicit by a definite negative: "But I do not allow a woman to teach or exercise authority over a man, but to remain quiet" (v. 12). That which is prohibited is teaching (*didaskein*) and having dominion (*authentein*).[1] The prohibition is not that a woman may not teach anyone (cf. Titus 2:3–4), but that within the church she must not teach and have authority over a man (*andros*).

It has been suggested that this prohibition applies only to wives, not to women in general.[2] It is true that the two Greek words used here for *man* and *woman* (*anēr* and *gunē*) can designate not only man and woman in general, but also husband and wife in particular.[3] However, there is no evidence in the larger context that the terms are meant to be restricted in the passage, or that they become more restricted in the verses under consideration. Contrariwise, the terms would seem to be meant more generally in verses 8–10 and, therefore, also in verses 11ff.

1. *Authentein* means to have authority over someone. For a detailed study of the meaning of the New Testament *hapax authentein* in the literature surrounding the time of the New Testament, see the author's article "AUTHENTEŌ in Reference to Women in 1 Timothy 2:12," *New Testament Studies* 30 (1984):143–57. In no case did the word have the negative or pejorative overtone of "domineer."
2. C. K. Barrett. *The Pastoral Epistles* (Oxford: Clarendon, 1963), p. 55.
3. See W. Bauer, W. F. Arndt, F. W. Gingrich, and F. W. Danker, *A Greek-English Lexicon of the New Testament and Other Early Christian Literature,* 2nd ed. rev. (Chicago: U. of Chicago, 1979), pp. 66–67, 168.

Thus the prohibition of the apostle has to do with maleness and femaleness, not just with the married estate or relationship.

The reason for such a vigorous prohibition ("I do not allow," *epitrepō*)[4] follows immediately in verses 13 and 14: "For it was Adam who was first created, and then Eve. And it was not Adam who was deceived, but the woman being quite deceived, fell into transgression." The first statement is that the order in which God created man and woman (Adam and Eve) expresses and determines the relationship God intended and the order of authority. The one formed first is to have dominion, the one formed after and from him is to be in subjection. Paul develops this argument and its implications in 1 Corinthians 11, and we shall turn to that passage shortly.

The second statement is related to the Fall and the fact that Eve (woman) was beguiled. Paul does not expand and develop this argument, and we must be content with his brief statement of it. One may only conjecture that the apostle cites this foundational incident to indicate that when the roles established by God in creation were reversed by Eve, it manifestly had a disastrous effect. It is noteworthy that no cultural reason is given or even alluded to in this passage; Paul gives instead only the most basic, foundational reason, one that is always germane to men and women—namely, God's creation order and the dire consequences of reversing the roles, as evidenced in the Fall. No

4. The word *epitrepō* is used three times by the apostle Paul (1 Cor. 14:34; 16:7; 1 Tim. 2:12). Two of the places (1 Cor. 14:34 and 1 Tim, 2:12) refer to the same issue—women speaking authoritatively or teaching in the church. The other (1 Cor. 16:7) refers to an action of the Lord. These three occurrences help determine the strength of the term's New Testament meaning, which has not been in doubt except for the present controversy and which is given by Bauer, Arndt, Gingrich, and Danker as "allow, permit" (*Greek-English Lexicon*, p. 303). Its usage by Paul with reference to the Lord in 1 Corinthians 16:7 demonstrates the term's strong sense of absoluteness. That this is the sense in 1 Corinthians 14:34 is made evident when Paul says in verse 37 that "the things which I write to you [including verse 34] are the Lord's commandment." Since 1 Corinthians 14:34 and 1 Timothy 2:12 use the same word about essentially the same subject, we may with confidence regard the "I do not allow" of 1 Timothy 2:12 as an expression by Paul of that which he regards as "the Lord's commandment."

more basic and binding reason could be cited. Paul thus follows the example of Jesus Christ who, when He dealt with the basic question of the permanence of the marriage relationship, cited the Father's creative action (cf. Matt. 19:3ff.).

1 CORINTHIANS 11:1–16

The reason Paul gives in 1 Timothy 2:13–14 is developed in 1 Corinthians 11:1–16. In 1 Corinthians 11, Paul discusses the freedom that the Corinthian women felt they had to abandon the order that God has ordained and expresses in nature.[5] Paul argues that our freedom in Christ does not allow us to overturn that order and the particular expression of it in Corinth and the apostolic age. But he is careful to insist at the end of his argument that God Himself has, by means of long hair, provided the covering needed. So he ends: "... but if a woman has long hair, it is a glory to her? For her hair is given to her for a covering" (1 Cor. 11:15). We thus have two things intertwined in this passage: the expression of the principle at stake in a particular practice, and the natural provision, long hair, that God has given and that expresses at all times the principle.

Paul begins his argument about the role relationship of men and women by placing it in the hierarchy of headships (*kephalē*).[6] "But I want you to understand that Christ is the head

5. Paul's use of the word *phusis* in verse 14 and in effect the argument from nature in verse 15 accords with his use of the word elsewhere. Of the word's eleven appearances in the New Testament, nine are in Paul's letters (Rom. 1:26; 2:14, 27; 11:21, 24; 1 Cor. 11:14; Gal. 2:15; 4:8; Eph. 2:3). The usage in Romans 1 and 2 most closely parallels the usage here. In Romans, nature is God's natural order, and to oppose nature is to oppose God's order (1:26). In Romans 2:14, doing the things of the law by nature is showing the work of God, who has written the work of the law on the heart.

6. *Kephalē* is used, "in the case of living beings, to denote superior rank.... The divine influence on the world results in the series: God the *kephalē* of Christ, Christ the *kephalē* of the man, man the *kephalē* of the woman" (Bauer, Arndt, Gingrich, and Danker, *Greek-English Lexicon*, p. 431). Cf. Heinrich Schlier, "*Kephalē*," in *Theological Dictionary of the New Testament*, ed. Gerhard Kittel and Gerhard Friedrich, trans. and ed. Geoffrey W. Bromiley, 9 vols. (Grand Rapids: Eerdmans, 1964–74)3:673–81, esp. pp. 679–

of every man, and the man is the head of a woman, and God is the head of Christ" (v. 3). He establishes the propriety of head-ship by appealing to that of Christ to man and God to Christ. At the same time, he shows that such headship is not derogatory to one's person, being, or essence. He sandwiches the disputed relation (that of man and woman) between undisputed ones to set it in a proper framework.

It needs to be noted that Paul speaks not only of Christ as the head and authority of every man, but also of God as the head of Christ. The headship of God the Father in relation to the incarnate Christ in no way detracts from or is detrimental to Christ's person as incarnate deity. His full deity, His being of the same essence as the Father, is not at all denied, nor must His deity be affirmed in such a way that the Father's headship must be denied to maintain it. The headship of God in reference to Christ can be readily seen and affirmed with no threat to Christ's identity. This chain of subordination with its implications is apparently given to help answer the objection some bring to the headship of man in reference to woman. Just as Christ is not a second-class person or deity because the Father is His head, so the woman is not a second-class person or human being because man is her head.

The apostle brings his argument to a focus by contrasting the glory (*doxa*), or reflection,[7] that the man and the woman each display. The man, he says, is the "glory of God," but the woman, the "glory of man" (v. 7). As verses 8–9 seem to indicate, that evaluation is based on the more immediate creation of Adam by God and the creation of Eve from and out of Adam. Thus, the woman will reflect and be the glory of the one from whom she was created, namely, man.[8] The argument is now

---

80. See especially Appendix 1 of this book by Wayne Grudem, "Does *kephalē* ('head') Mean 'Source' or 'Authority Over' in Greek Literature? A Survey of 2,336 Examples."

7. See Bauer, Arndt, Gingrich, and Danker, *Greek-English Lexicon*, p. 203.

8. "The same point emerges from vv. 8f., where the being of woman as *doxa* . . . is explained by the fact that the origin and *raison d'etre* of woman are to be found in man. Hence, man is the image and reflection of God to the degree that in his created being he points directly to God as Creator.

advanced in verses 8–10 on the grounds of the order of creation of man and woman and the significance of this order for the headship of man in reference to woman. "For man does not originate from [*ek*] woman; but woman from [*ex*] man" (v. 8). The significance of this order, also referred to in 1 Timothy 2:13, is now stated in verse 9: "For indeed man was not created for [*dia*] the woman's sake, but woman for [*dia*][9] the man's sake." Here the apostle cites the order of creation explicit in Genesis 2:18–25 and the reason for woman's creation—to be a help to man (v. 18)—to establish and define the divinely determined role relationship. To put it in a composite of words from Genesis and 1 Corinthians, man was not created to help and be the helper of woman, but woman was created to help and be the helper of man. This order is not based on the Fall and the curse (see Gen. 3:16), but on the order of God's creation (contra Krister Stendahl and many others).[10] Paul concludes this section by saying that this order ought to be in evidence "because of the angels" (v. 10), apparently referring to the supernatural beings who desire to see God's order preserved and God's glory displayed.[11]

Lest Paul's argument for the role relationship be misunderstood, he quickly adds in verses 11 and 12, as Peter does in 1 Peter 3:7, the equality and natural interdependence of man and woman. These verses indicate that the order referred to in verses 8 and 9 does not glorify man but teaches that "all things

---

Woman is the reflection of man to the degree that in her created being she points to man. . . . In this relation of man and woman we are dealing with the very foundations of their creaturehood." Schlier, "Kephalē," *Theological Dictionary of the New Testament,* 3:679.

9. *Dia* with the accusative means "because of, on account of, for the sake of." See Bauer, Arndt, Gingrich, and Danker, *Greek-English Lexicon,* p. 181; Albrecht Oepke, "*Dia,*" in *Theological Dictionary of the New Testament,* 2:69; and the standard Greek grammars.

10. Cf., for example, Krister Stendahl, *The Bible and the Role of Women* (Philadelphia: Fortress, 1966), p. 29.

11. See F. F. Bruce, *1 and 2 Corinthians* (London: Oliphants, 1971), p. 106 and the reference cited there. See also J. A. Fitzmyer, "A Feature of Qumran Angelology and the Angels of 1 Cor. 11:10," *New Testament Studies* 4 (1957–58):48ff.

originate from God" (v. 12). So the concept of mutual dependence in the Lord is added to give balance and prevent false glorying or misunderstanding, not to negate the previous argument. Here again, the role relationship of man and woman and their mutual dependence can be correlated without one concept destroying the other.

Some have said that it is not man and woman that are here spoken of, but only husband and wife.[12] Again, that understanding is hardly likely. That is most clearly indicated by the fact that the relationship in view between the man and woman in verses 11 and 12 is not that of husband and wife, but of parent and child, which seems to imply that throughout the passage the words have been used in the more general sense of man and woman, not husband and wife. There are also other indications.[13]

12. Cf., for example, the translation of 1 Corinthians 11:3 in the RSV— "husband." Note that the NEB and the NIV returned to the more general usage, "man."
13. Ralph H. Alexander gives these considerations for regarding the passage as referring to men and women in general rather than to husbands and wives in particular: "Crucial for the proper interpretation of our passage is the determination as to whether the terms are employed here to refer to husband and wife, or man and woman. The latter sense has been accepted for the following reasons: (1) This is the normal usage of the two terms. (2) *Anēr* is the more popular term employed to translate *ish* in the LXX, though *anthrōpos* is often employed as well. (3) Verse 3 qualifies *andros* with *pantos* ('every') which would tend to indicate all men, not just husbands. (4) The anarthrous *gunaikos* stresses the nature, character, or essence of a woman in verse 3. If 'wife' were meant, the article would be more appropriate in order to identify, or specify, *the* wife of the man. *Anēr* is definite when related to the woman in order to signify *the* head, as is true of all three authority relationships. (5) Verse 4 employs the word 'all' when speaking of *anēr* and verse 5 does the same with *gunē*. This inclusive adjective along with the participles for prophesying and praying would tend to indicate that men and women in general are involved, not just husbands and wives. What would unmarrieds do when they pray and prophesy? (6) Verses 7–11 are concerned with creation as a basis for the regulations given. This, in turn, would tend to stress men and women in general rather than just husbands and wives. Verses 11–12 speak of the mutual interdependence of the sexes in the process of procreation. If husband and wife were meant, these verses would be illogical, for the husband does not come into being through the wife nor is the wife the source of the husband. (7) Verses 13–16 argue from nature, which would give greater support that man and woman in general is being discussed,

A most striking one is that in verses 13–16, Paul appeals to nature, and what is true in or by nature applies not just to husbands and wives, but to men and women in general.

Finally, it is imperative to take account of the fact, evident in most of the passages under consideration, that the apostle himself regards the teaching as not limited to the local situation: "But if one is inclined to be contentious, we have no other practice, nor have the churches of God" (v. 16).

1 CORINTHIANS 14:33B–38

We turn now to 1 Corinthians 14:33*b*(or 34)–38. These verses come in the midst of a chapter in which the apostle authoritatively regulates the use of spiritual gifts according to the norms "Let all things be done for edification" (v. 26) and "Let all things be done properly and in an orderly manner" (v. 40). He requires any man who speaks (*lalei*) in a tongue to keep silent (*sigatō*, v. 28) unless there is one to interpret, and then only two, or at the most three, may speak in turn. Likewise the prophets are to speak (*laleitōsan*) in turn, and if another is given a revelation, the first is to keep silent (*sigatō*, vv. 29–30). It is this section dealing with speaking and silence that provides the setting for Paul to speak about matters in regard to women, using the same two key words (*laleō* and (*sigatō*). And just as the order of God, who is not a God of confusion but of peace (v. 33), must prevail for tongues speakers and prophets, so it must prevail for women.

The speaking prohibited to women in verse 34 and the silence demanded is to be interpreted by two factors. First, the speaking (*laleō*) must be, considering the light of the immediate context and previous usage, public communication (cf. vv. 27, 29). Second, the correlation of speaking and silence found here is paralleled in 1 Timothy 2:11–14, where what is prohibited is women teaching men. Such an understanding seems most ap-

---

rather than just husbands and wives." "An Exegetical Presentation on 1 Corinthians 11:2–16 and 1 Timothy 2:8–15" (typescript of paper presented at the Seminar on Women in the Ministry, Western Conservative Baptist Seminary, November 1976), pp. 5–6.

propriate for 1 Corinthians 14. Therefore, women are prohibited from speaking in church because it would violate the role relationship between men and women that God has established. In the event that the prohibition against speaking and teaching in the church be circumvented by women who say that they are only asking questions and learning, the apostle points in verse 35 to another solution that clearly will not violate the prohibition of verse 34.

Now we need to note the reasons for this prohibition. The appeal is to the need for subjection (*hypotassesthōsan*, v. 34), which would be violated by speaking. This subjection is taught by "the Law" (*ho nomos*, v. 34). It is most likely that "the Law" refers to God's law, and to the same passage cited in 1 Timothy 2:11ff. and 1 Corinthians 11:1ff.—namely, the creation order described in Genesis 2. The violation of the subjection taught in God's law is what makes it shameful[14] (v. 35) for a woman to speak in the church. The apostle rebukes any disobedience by asking in verse 36: "Was it from you that the word of God first went forth? Or has it come to you only?" With these pointed and crisp questions, Paul shows that the Corinthians must not suppose that they originated God's Word and order, or that they alone have some word from God contrary to the understanding and practice of the apostle and all the other churches.

Although it is true that the word *woman* used in 1 Corinthians 14 is particularly applied to wives in verse 35, it must still be asked whether Paul intends the prohibition to include married women alone, and thus to exclude single women. Considering the parallel passages—1 Corinthians 11 and especially 1 Timothy 2—it seems more likely that Paul does not intend to restrict the prohibition to married women. He simply refers in verse 35 to the concrete example of married women— which most of the women in the congregation were—to provide a guideline for other and different situations from that of the married relationship.

Let us set this section concerning women speaking or

14. *Aischron*, the same word used in 1 Corinthians 11:6.

teaching in church in its context–a chapter on spiritual gifts. Apparently some people, then as now, claimed that if a person has a spiritual gift, he can use it in the church without restriction; the gift is from the Spirit, and who can impose order on what God gives? The apostle argues that God is a God of peace and not of confusion, that He wants things done in a proper and orderly manner, and therefore that an unrestricted use of the gifts is contrary to God. In this chapter on spiritual gifts, the apostle also refutes the apparent assertion that unless women are allowed to speak and thus teach in church, the church may oppose God and His Spirit. He says that such an exercise of that spiritual gift is contrary to God's order of creation (cf. "the Law," that is, the Old Testament teaching of Genesis 2), and that no appeal to spiritual gifts or freedom can set this aside. Later he explains how women may use that gift in teaching women and children (Titus 2), but here he simply refutes an erroneous appeal to the Spirit and spiritual gifts.

Finally, we need again to recognize the authority with which the apostle gives this teaching and the application of it to all the churches, not just to Corinth. In reference to the former, he self-consciously categorizes this teaching as the commandment of the Lord ("The things which I write to you are the Lord's commandment," v. 37). In reference to the latter, the apostle puts the teachings of this chapter in the most absolute and universal perspective. He asserts the principle that God is not a God of confusion but of peace (v. 33*a*), then adds, "as in all the churches of the saints" (v. 33*b*). Verse 33*b* might, instead of concluding the sentence that begins in verse 31, begin verse 34. But whether it belongs grammatically to verses 31–33*a* or to verse 34, the lesson is clear that the teachings of the chapter as a whole, and the teaching concerning women in particular, apply to all the churches.

CONCLUSION

We conclude from our survey of these three key passages that the apostle Paul laid down a universally normative regulation that prohibits women from ruling and teaching men in the church. These passages are not illustrations but commands; the commands are grounded not in time-bound, historically and culturally relative arguments that apply only to Paul's day and age, but in the way God created man and woman to relate to each other.

The creation order and its correlatives of headship and subjection appear in each passage, just as that order and its correlatives provide the one and only foundation for the role relationship in marriage. To dismiss the role relationship in the church's teaching-ruling function as simply cultural would carry with it the dismissal of the analogous role relationship in marriage as also cultural, because they are based on the same principle. Letha Scanzoni and Nancy Hardesty do just that,[15] and so does Paul K. Jewett.[16] Likewise, if one preserves the role relationship in marriage because of the creation order, one also must preserve the role relationship in the church's teaching-ruling function, because it is based on that same creation order.

The fact that "there is neither male nor female, for you are all one in Christ Jesus" (Gal. 3:28) does not deny the teaching of 1 Timothy 2 and 1 Corinthians 14, just as it does not deny man's maleness and woman's femaleness, nor annul their relationship in the family (cf. Eph. 5:22ff.).

The exclusion of women from the teaching and ruling office and functions of the church in 1 Timothy 2:11–15 and 1 Corinthians 14:33b–37 must not be construed as all the New Testament evidence on the role of women in the church, even though it is very specific. Several passages indicate that women are involved in diaconal tasks and appropriate teaching situations. A sampling of those activities may be seen in the following: older women are called upon to teach and train younger women concerning their responsibilities to their husbands and children

---

15. Compare the two chapters "Love, Honor and _____?" and "Living in Partnership" in *All We're Meant to Be* (Waco, Tex.: Word, 1974), pp. 88–117. Also see the term *equalitarian marriage* on p. 118 and elsewhere.
16. *Man as Male and Female* (Grand Rapids: Eerdmans, 1975), pp. 137–41 ("Female Subordination and the Bond of Marriage").

(Titus 2:3–5); wives (*gunaikas*) are referred to in the midst of the description of male deacons (1 Tim. 3:11); Phoebe is designated "a servant [*diakonon*] of the church which is at Cenchrea" (Rom. 16:1); Paul refers in 1 Corinthians to women praying or prophesying (11:5); and Priscilla and Aquila, that inseparable husband-and-wife team, in a discreet and private meeting expound to Apollos "the way of God more accurately" (Acts 18:26).

Therefore, in considering the ministry of men and women in the church, three biblical truths must be held in correlation: (1) Men and women equally bear God's image: "there is neither male nor female; for you are all one in Christ Jesus" (Gal. 3:28). Therefore, men and women are, in and before Christ, equal. (2) Men and women manifest in their sexuality a difference created and ordered by God. By this creative order, women are to be subject to men in the church and are therefore excluded from the ruling-teaching office and functions (1 Tim. 2:11–15; 1 Cor. 14:33b–37; cf. 1 Tim. 3:4–5), which men alone are to fill. And (3) women have a function to fulfill in the diaconal task, of the church and in the teaching of women and children (cf., e.g., 1 Tim. 3:11; Titus 2:3–4; Rom. 16:1).

OBJECTIONS ANSWERED

Several objections have been raised against the traditional interpretation of 1 Timothy 2:11–15 and 1 Corinthians 11:1–16, and to these we now turn.

"THE STATEMENT OF PAUL IN 1 TIMOTHY 2:13—'FOR IT WAS ADAM WHO WAS FIRST CREATED, AND THEN EVE'—IS NOT SIGNIFICANT FOR THE ROLE RELATIONSHIP OF MEN AND WOMEN."

Scanzoni and Hardesty say, "If beings created first are to have precedence, then the animals are clearly our betters."[17] The point of Paul's statement, however, is not merely that of chronology but that of derivation and relationship, as his fuller handling

17. *All We're Meant to Be*, p. 28; cf. also Paul K. Jewett, *Man as Male and Female*, pp. 126–27.

of the Old Testament episode in 1 Corinthians 11:8–9 shows. The recognition of that point removes the objection of Scanzoni and Hardesty because mankind in general, or man and woman in particular, are not made from the animals. Nor is man derived from the dust of the ground as if shaped or fashioned from a living entity (contra Paul K. Jewett). The Old Testament narrative says, "The LORD God fashioned [built] into a woman the rib which He had taken from the man" (Gen. 2:22). We see that Paul is concerned with origin, not with mere chronology, when we read the exegetical language of 1 Corinthians 11:8–9: "For man does not originate from woman, but woman from man; for indeed man was not created for the woman's sake, but woman for the man's sake."

"PAUL'S EXEGESIS OF GENESIS 2:18FF. IN 1 CORINTHIANS 11:1–16 IS INACCURATE."

When Paul sees in Genesis 2 an order of authority between the man and woman, says Jewett, Paul is exhibiting not what Genesis says or implies, but a remnant of his rabbinic thinking.[18]

The way in which woman is made out of man is highly significant for the relationship of man and woman, as seen not only in the Pauline texts, but also in the text of Genesis itself: "And the man said, 'This is now bone of my bones, and flesh of my flesh; she shall be called Woman, because she was taken out of Man'" (Gen. 2:23). In addition, the next verse says: "For this cause a man shall leave his father and his mother, and shall cleave to his wife; and they shall become one flesh." Not only for Paul but also for Adam and Moses—as well as for God, who created woman in such a way and evoked the responses and principial applications—the created order and relationship is a most important factor in how man regards woman, how woman regards man, and how both regard their relationship to each other. The relationship of woman to man, as well as their cohumanity, comes through eloquently in the play on words in

---

18. *Man as Male and Female,* p. 119. (Read this in the context of pp. 111–19.)

Genesis 2:23: "She shall be called Woman [*ishah*], because she was taken out of Man [*ish*]."

> The woman is created for him out of his very being and the man names his new companion "woman." We see here the difference in function between man and woman. In Hebrew thought name-giving is "the prerogative of a superior" (J. A. Motyer, *New Bible Dictionary*). God exercises this prerogative in Genesis 1, giving names to the things He has created. Man shares in this when he names the animals over whom he has been given dominion by God. So when God brings the woman to the man and he gives her her name he is demonstrating his God-given headship and responsibility. Yet in that very act the oneness and harmony that should exist between men and women is also illustrated. To quote again from Motyer, "When the name-giver places his own name upon the person named, the giving of the name signifies the joining of two hitherto separate persons in the closest unity." Adam's name in Hebrew is "*ish*" and he called the woman "*ishah*," which is the feminine form of his own name.[19]

God's creation of woman from man provides the basis for woman and man becoming one flesh in marriage: "For this cause a man ... shall cleave to his wife; and they shall become one flesh" (v. 24).

It is prejudicial to assert that creation should not provide, as Paul says it does, a basis for the relationship of men and women, for when the episode occurred and then when it was first recorded—under the inspiration of God's Spirit—its theological significance was vigorously affirmed. What Paul says in 1 Corinthians 11:8–9 is quite evidently the fact of the matter. Verse 8 affirms that man was not created out of or from woman,

19. Bob Key and Daphne Key, *Adam, Eve, and Equality* (Leicester: Universities and Colleges Christian Fellowship, 1976), p. 7. The article cited in this quotation is "Name," in *The New Bible Dictionary*, ed. J. D. Douglas (Grand Rapids: Eerdmans, 1962), pp. 861–64. Motyer also says, "When a superior thus exercised his authority, the giving of the name signified the appointment of the person named to some specific position, function, or relationship" (p. 862).

but woman out of and from man. Similarly, verse 9 affirms that man was not created for (to be a helper of) woman, but woman for man. That furnishes the scriptural basis for Paul's affirmation in verse 3 that the man is the head of the woman. He is saying, in effect, that if one human being is created to be the helper of another human being, the one who receives such a helper has a certain authority over the helper. It is said in opposition to this that because sometimes in the Old Testament God is called man's "helper" (the same Hebrew word is used of God that is used of woman), this argument cannot be valid. Cannot a word have a different nuance when applied to God from what it has when applied to human beings? Certainly a different nuance or connotation of a word does not nullify the apostolic exegesis and application.

Furthermore, contrary to Jewett's argument that Paul's exegesis is inaccurate is this fact: The order of authority Paul discerns in Genesis 2 is presumed in Genesis 3, lying behind the judgment of God on man's sin. Genesis 3 presumes the reality of childbearing (Gen. 1:28), in which the woman will now experience the effects of the Fall and sin (3:16). It presumes the reality of work (Gen. 1:28; 2:15), in which the man will now experience the effects of the Fall and sin (3:17ff.). and it presumes the reality of the role relationship between wife and husband established by God's creation order in Genesis 2:18ff., a relationship that will now experience the effects of the Fall and sin (3:16). "He shall rule over you" expresses the effects of sin corrupting the relationship of husband (the head) and wife. Just as childbearing and work were established before the Fall and were corrupted by it, so this relationship existed before the Fall and was corrupted by it. Neither childbearing, nor work, nor the role relationship of wife and husband is being introduced in Genesis 3; all are previously existing realities that have been affected by the Fall. If Genesis 3 can so readily presume that an order of authority between man and woman has been established in Genesis 2, surely it is erroneous to say that Genesis 2 does not and cannot teach what Paul says it does.

"THE ROLE RELATIONSHIP OF MAN AND WOMAN IN MARRIAGE AND
THE CHURCH IS BASED SOLELY UPON THE EFFECTS OF SIN AND THE
FALL (E.G., GEN. 3:16)."

Proponents of this point of view go on to say that just as we try to alleviate the effects of sin on childbirth with anesthesia and the effects of sin on work with air-conditioned tractors, so we should alleviate the effects of sin on the man-woman relationship by eliminating the headship of man. I have two points to make in response to this argument.

First, I agree that we should seek to relieve the effects of the Fall and sin in all three of those areas. But we should not do so by eliminating childbirth, work, and the role relationship of man and woman. Rather, we should alleviate that which corrupts those three entities. With respect to the latter, the apostles urge husbands to love, honor, and not be bitter toward their wives; they do not urge them to cease being the head of their households (cf. Eph. 5:22ff.; 1 Pet. 3:1ff.; Col. 3:18–19). The removal of a husband's oppressive rule over his wife is not the removal of his headship over her or of their role relationship to each other; it is the removal, through love, of the effects of sin on the role relationship.

Second, the Bible never builds its case for the role relationship of men and women in marriage upon the effects of sin manifested in Genesis 3:16. The apostle Paul appeals to the pre-Fall creation order as normative. (See Eph. 5:31; 1 Cor. 11:8–9; 14:34; 1 Tim. 2:13–14; the "law" referred to or quoted in these places is Gen. 2, not Gen. 3.) It is true that in 1 Timothy 2:14, Paul also refers to the Fall after citing the creation order, but he does this to show the dire consequences of reversing the creation order on this most historic and significant occasion. God's creation order for men and women, not the fallen order, is normative for the New Testament.

"PAUL REFERS IN 1 CORINTHIANS 11:5 TO WOMEN PRAYING AND
PROPHESYING IN THE CHURCH. EITHER PAUL THERE CONTRADICTS
HIS INJUNCTIONS TO WOMEN TO KEEP SILENT IN CHURCH (1 COR.
14:34; 1 TIM. 2:11–12),[20] OR 1 CORINTHIANS 11:5 MUST GOVERN OUR
INTERPRETATION OF 1 CORINTHIANS 14:34 AND 1 TIMOTHY 2:11–12."[21]

A problem with this objection is that the latter two passages
are clearly the didactic passages on the subject, while
1 Corinthians 11 only mentions the subject incidentally. Therefore, our interpretation of 1 Corinthians 14 and 1 Timothy 2
ought to govern our interpretation of 1 Corinthians 11, not vice
versa. It also is appropriate to assume that the great apostle Paul
does not contradict himself in the same letter and only a few
chapters apart.

Several reasonable ways to integrate these passages have
been proposed: (1) The praying and prophesying mentioned in
1 Corinthians 11 did not occur in the church.[22] Some would add
that in 1 Timothy 2, Paul limits to men the activity of praying in
the church.[23] (2) The praying and prophesying mentioned in
1 Corinthians 11 occurred in the church, but by mentioning the

---

20. Krister Stendahl, *The Bible and the Role of Women*, p. 35. Eduard Schweizer
    says that the verses in question in 1 Corinthians 14 are a later interpolation
    and that they are contradicted by 1 Corinthians 11:5 ("The Service of
    Worship: An Exposition of 1 Corinthians 14," *Interpretation* 13 [1959]:
    400ff). Although there is a slight textual problem, it is a matter not of the
    verses' (34–35) being interpolated into the text, but of their being in the
    proper place. Kurt Aland et al. in their textual apparatus enumerate the
    very strong textual witnesses to these verses' belonging in the usually
    acknowledged position, giving this textual reading a *B*-level evaluation.
    (*The Greek New Testament*, 3d ed. [London: United Bible Societies, 1975],
    p. 611). For the basis of their judgment, see Bruce M. Metzger, ed., *A
    Textual Commentary on the Greek New Testament* (London: United Bible
    Societies, 1971), p. 565.
21. For example, Irene M. Robbins, "St. Paul and the Ministry of Women,"
    Expository Times 44 (1935): 196.
22. For example, Charles Hodge, *An Exposition of the First Epistle to the
    Corinthians* (New York: Carter, 1857), p. 305.
23. For example, Charles C. Ryrie, *The Place of Women in the Church* (New York:
    Macmillan, 1958), p. 76.

practice Paul does not condone it.[24] He refers to the practice in order to get at the issue with which he is dealing in chapter 11; he returns to the practice in chapter 14 and forbids women from praying and prophesying in the church.[25] Paul deals with the practice of eating meat in an idol's temple in an analogous way: in 1 Corinthians 8:10, he mentions the practice with seeming approval, but in 1 Corinthians 10:20–22, he appears to forbid it.[26] And (3) women may pray and prophesy[27] in the church because those activities are expressly allowed in 1 Corinthians 11.[28] I regard the third solution as the correct one. If that is correct, then it must be recognized that the apostle regards praying and prophesying on the one hand, and speaking that involves teaching (cf. again 1 Cor. 14:34 and 1 Tim. 2:12) on the other hand, as distinguishable and different activities. Praying publicly in the midst of others does not imply or involve any authority or headship over others. Likewise prophesying, an activity in which the one prophesying is essentially a passive instrument through which God communicates, does not necessarily imply or involve an authority or headship of the one prophesying over others.

What 1 Corinthians 14 and 1 Timothy 2 forbid, then, is authoritative speaking, teaching, and ruling. As is apparent, all three solutions preserve the didactic element in 1 Corinthians 14 and 1 Timothy 2 and are consistent with the interpretation of those passages that we have already put forth.

24. For a possible example, see Archibald Robertson and Alfred Plummer, *1 Corinthians*, 2d ed. (Edinburgh: Clark, 1914), pp. 324–25.
25. R. St. John Parry, *The First Epistle of Paul the Apostle to the Corinthians* (Cambridge: Cambridge U., 1926), pp. 210–11.
26. Hodge, p. 148.
27. I am persuaded by a study of prophecy in the New Testament (expressed by the terms *prophēteia, prophēteuō,* and *prophētēs*) that this activity is the result of God's Spirit acting in and through a person to produce a revelation, and that this is intrinsically different from what the New Testament means by teaching and preaching. Although that conclusion might affect one's choice between the three solutions being offered, it will remain true apart from one's choice.
28. J. B. Hurley, "Did Paul Require Veils or the Silence of Women? A Consideration of 1 Cor. 11:2–16 and 1 Cor. 14:33b–36," *Westminster Theological Journal* 35 (1973): 203.

"TO AFFIRM THE TRADITIONAL INTERPRETATION OF THESE PASSAGES IS TO EXCLUDE WOMEN AND THEIR GIFTS FROM SERVICE IN THE LIFE OF THE CHURCH. SUCH AN ERRONEOUS DEDUCTION MUST BE REPUDIATED ON THE BASIS OF CLEAR BIBLICAL TEACHING."

Although the New Testament teaching about marriage is presented in terms of man as the head over his wife and family, no one deduces from that truth that the wife is not vitally involved, performing many exceedingly important and necessary functions in the marriage and the family. Her gifts and graces have free range except when and where they impinge upon the headship of her husband. The same is true in the church. The exclusion of women from the ruling and teaching offices and functions in the church does not mean that women have no place of service in the church. The teaching and ruling offices and functions are not the only gifts, functions, or services in the church. Just as in marriage and the family, so also in the church the activities and functions of women are necessary and important. No part of the body of Christ (especially men, in this case) may say of another part, "I have no need of you" (1 Cor. 12:21). And no part of the Body of Christ (especially women, in this case) may say that because they are not occupying the office or performing the function of a leader, they are not a significant part of the body (cf. 1 Cor. 12:14–20). The truth of God through the apostle Paul is exceedingly important in our context: "But now God has placed the members, each one of them, in the body, just as He desired" (1 Cor. 12:18).

The New Testament tells of women being involved in the ministry and life of the church in various ways, but always in ways other than the teaching-ruling offices and functions. References to women granting Jesus assistance in His ministry, and to His interaction with them, are well known and need no documentation. It is certainly noteworthy that women were present at the cross and empty tomb, and that women were the first to announce the resurrection. The apostle Paul designates certain women as those "who have shared my struggle in the cause of the gospel" and as "fellow-workers" (Phil. 4:3). In Titus 2:3–5,

Paul urges the older women to teach (within the church) the younger women, to exhort "the young women to love their husbands, to love their children, to be sensible, pure, workers at home, kind, being subject to their own husbands, that the word of God may not be dishonored." Older widows are to be enrolled in a special order in the church, apparently both to serve (cf. v. 13) and to receive care and remuneration; they are to be enrolled on the basis of their previous service in the church (1 Tim. 5:9ff., esp. v. 10). But at the same time, Paul opposed such an order for younger widows, preferring that they return to the condition that expresses their basic inclination and need— namely, the marital state and its privileges and responsibilities. (Men and women who do not have the inclination and need to be married—namely, those who have a gift from God to be single—he encourages to be single as an avenue of service, but not as a condition for church office [cf. 1 Cor. 7]).

One of the most interesting references to women or wives in the midst of a discussion of church officers is in 1 Timothy 3:11: "Women must likewise be dignified, not malicious gossips, but temperate, faithful in all things." My opinion is that women are mentioned and their qualifications given in this passage because they are to be involved in the diaconal activities. They are not mentioned in the midst of the description of bishops because women are excluded from the ruling-teaching office. They are mentioned in the midst of the description of deacons because it is perfectly proper for them to be involved in the diaconal ministry, which does not involve, inherently, ruling and teaching. It is also striking that the office of deacon is described not in both male and female terms or without any reference to sex, but in male terms, and the reference to women or wives appears in the midst of that description. It would seem, therefore, that the office of deacon is an office for men only, but that at the same time women are to be involved in the diaconal area. Thus, I would encourage churches to have the deacons' wives (the most likely meaning of the word in 1 Tim. 3:11, see the NIV) help the deacons.

The significance of bishops and deacons being described as males may be challenged on the grounds that they also are described as being husbands and fathers. It could be insisted that if marriage and parenthood are not norms for officers (both bachelors and husbands without children are elected to such offices), then neither is maleness a norm. Here again, Scripture must interpret Scripture. How does the church know that the apostle is describing officers in terms of the usual situation—marriage and a family—indicating that the way a man lives in that situation demonstrates his ability, and not mandating that officers be married and have children? It is possible that God would require such qualifications for office—compare some of the stringent requirements for office in the Old Testament! The answer is that the teaching of our Lord in Matthew 19:11–12 and the teaching of the apostle Paul in 1 Corinthians 7 (and his application of that teaching in 1 Cor. 9:5 to himself as an apostle—an office that includes the concepts of elder or bishop [cf. 1 Pet. 5:1; 2 John 1; 3 John 1]) indicates that marriage and children are not necessary for the officer. Why, then, does the apostle describe the offices in terms of married men with families? He does so because that was the usual situation for most men (cf. again 1 Cor. 9:5) and because a man's conduct in the marriage and family situation serves as one of the best indicators of his qualifications for office.

As for the offices' being described in male terms, the case is otherwise. For one thing, women are prohibited in 1 Timothy 2:12 from teaching and ruling men. Furthermore, the emphasis on man's headship in the home (1 Tim. 3:4–5, 12) is correlated with man's responsibility and, in the case of the elder, with his authority in the church. That headship is a constant keynote in New Testament teaching on the role relationship of men and women and is constantly affirmed as the male responsibility. Finally, women (or wives) are self-consciously mentioned and distinguished from the men and the offices mentioned (1 Tim. 3:11). These considerations would seem to indicate that the male terminology is not in the same category as the marriage and family terminology. We may then draw the following conclusions: On the one hand, Scripture shows the terms concerning marriage and the family to be relative, not absolute; on the other hand, the terms concerning maleness are specifically supported and demanded in Scripture and are, therefore, not relative.

The case of Phoebe. That leads us to consider Phoebe, the *diakonos* "of the church which is at Cenchrea" (Rom. 16:1–2). The first consideration is the meaning of *diakonos* in this context. This word is the common Greek word for servant (cf. John 2:5, 9). Christ is designated as a servant by this term (Rom. 15:8); the state is called a servant (Rom. 13:4); Christians are called servants of Christ and God (cf. John 12:26). Because the model for leadership in the church is the servant Jesus, and because leadership is manifested in service, those leaders are called servants or ministers by means of this Greek word (cf. Matt. 20:26; Mark 10:43; 1 Cor. 3:5; 2 Cor. 3:6; 6:4; Eph. 3:7; 6:21; Col. 1:7, 23, 25; 4:7; 1 Thess. 3:2; 1 Tim. 4:6). Paul speaks of himself and others in these passages as servants or ministers of Christ, of God, and of the church. Finally, the word is specially and specifically applied to those officers of the church whose task is primarily if not exclusively service—namely, the deacons, who bear this Greek word as their title, in distinction from the bishops (cf. Phil. 1:1; 1 Tim. 3:1, 8, 12).

The question is, in what sense is the term used in reference to Phoebe? The vast majority of modern English translations have not translated this term "minister" or "deacon" in reference to Phoebe, because they want to express what they think Paul meant by the term. Even though the term is translated "minister" in reference to Paul and others as leaders of the church, since Paul himself has ruled women out of the teaching-ruling offices, it is necessary to translate *diakonos* here by something other than "minister." Furthermore, in the passage where the term *diakonos* (translated "deacon") designates one special office, it is applied self-consciously to men but not to women (women are distinguished from deacons in this passage); out of regard for Paul's usage of this term, translators will not use the term "deacon" in reference to Phoebe the woman (cf. 1 Tim. 3:8ff., esp. v. 12). Phoebe, then, served in some very special and significant capacity of service in the church, but she was not a "deacon" in the official sense of the term.

Even if one were to translate *diakonos* in reference to Phoebe as "deacon," it would in no way overturn or alter the clear teaching of the apostle Paul in 1 Timothy 2:12, which is that a woman is not to teach or exercise authority over a man—that is, she is not to serve in ruling and teaching offices or functions.

The second consideration with reference to Phoebe is the meaning of *prostatis* in Romans 16:2: " . . . she herself has also been a helper [*prostatis*] of many, and of myself as well." The argument is that the word *prostatis* indicates that she was a ruler or had oversight in the church. It is true that the masculine form of this word (*prostatēs*) means "one who stands before, front-rank man, . . . leader, chief,"[29] but the feminine form, which is used here of Phoebe, means "protectress, patroness, helper."[30] So the argument turns more on the significance of the masculine form of the word than on the feminine form, which is the one used here. An analogy may help to show the danger of this kind of argument. The Greek word *presbyteros* in its masculine form can mean either "an older man" or "a leader in the church, an elder"; but the feminine form of the term, *presbytera*, certainly does not mean "church officer" or "elder" as well as "old woman" (cf. 1 Tim. 5:2). Surely Jewett understands the term *prostatis* correctly when he says that its use in reference to Phoebe "should hardly be taken to mean that Phoebe was a woman 'ruler.' Rather the meaning would seem to be that she was one who cared for the affairs of others by aiding them with her resources."[31]

The case of Prisca. Finally, we turn to one of the most illustrious women in the New Testament church—Prisca (or

29. H. G. Liddell and Robert Scott, *A Greek-English Lexicon*, 9th ed. (New York: Oxford, 1940), p. 1526.
30. Bauer, Arndt, Gingrich, and Danker, *Greek-English Lexicon*, p. 718.
31. *Man as Male and Female*, p. 170.

Priscilla), the wife of Aquila (Acts 18:2, 18, 26; Rom. 16:3; 1 Cor. 16:19; 2 Tim. 4:19). Several things stand out about Prisca. She and her husband are named together, and her name is often first. Almost wherever they are, a church meets in their house (Rom. 16:5; 1 Cor. 16:19). They are both called Paul's "fellow-workers in Christ Jesus" (Rom. 16:3). And both of them take Apollos aside and explain to him "the way of God more accurately" (Acts 18:26). Full weight must be given to all that is said of her, and especially of whatever part she had in the personal and private ministry that she and Aquila exercised toward Apollos. But this personal and private ministry with her husband ("they," not "she," took Apollos aside) in no way negates the teaching of the New Testament that excludes a woman from a public ministry of teaching and ruling in the church (cf. again 1 Tim. 2:12).

CONCLUSION

Two facts emerge. The first is that none of the passages recognizing and encouraging women in their service in the church recognize or encourage them in the public and authoritative teaching-ruling offices or functions in reference to the church as a whole or to men in particular. The data has reinforced, not minimized or refuted, that teaching. The second fact is that the New Testament and the apostles do recognize and encourage women to use their gifts in various other capacities in the life and service of the church. Those two facts must be seen in correlation, and neither should be used to negate or overturn the other.

When one seeks to determine the areas and functions in which the gifts of women are utilized in the church, one finds that almost every area or function is in view except that which is specifically prohibited. Women pray and prophesy, and women perform various diaconal tasks and functions. The area of activity most often emphasized is that of diaconal service (cf. again 1 Tim. 3:11 in context; Rom. 16:1-2; 1 Tim. 5:10ff.). I would encourage churches to have the deacons' wives (the most likely meaning of the word in 1 Tim. 3:11, see the NIV) help the deacons. And even teaching and exercising authority are ruled out only when they involve the church as a whole or men in particular. Women are urged to teach other women in the church (Tit. 2:3–5) and to exercise authority, under their husbands, over the household or home. (In 1 Tim. 5:14, "keep house" means literally, "manage one's household.") And it is evident that in a home where there is no father, the mother is the head. These considerations point up the fact that the Bible is not saying or implying that women are inherently incapable of engaging in or exercising those gifts, but that God has ordained a role relationship between equals, men and women, in these areas of authority and leadership, giving to man the role of head.

Christians and churches faithful to Scripture and to the Creator-Redeemer who reveals His will in Scripture should encourage both the role relationship of men and women that God ordains and the free exercise, in harmony with the role relationship, of the gifts He gives to both men and women.

4

Conclusion

TWO GENERAL OBJECTIONS

Two objections raised against the church's traditional view of the relationship of men and women relate to both marriage and the church, so we have waited until now to discuss them. One objection is of a philosophical nature, the other theological.

"SUBORDINATION OR SUBMISSION THAT RESTS ON THE FACT OF WOMAN'S FEMININITY IS INTRINSICALLY ANTITHETICAL TO EQUALITY AND NECESSARILY IMPLIES INFERIORITY."

But the New Testament insists, in opposition to Jewett and others,[1] that subordination does not imply inferiority, even if the aspect of "ontology"—namely, femininity—is brought into the picture (cf. 1 Cor. 11:3). The apostle Paul in his appeal to the relation of God the Father to God the Son does not regard Christ's Sonship and resultant incarnation as implying His inferiority to the Father. Although Christ the Son's submission is expressed in the areas of action and of incarnation (the areas of

---

1. *Man as Male and Female* (Grand Rapids: Eerdmans, 1975), p. 131.

service and of the accomplishment of salvation; cf. also 1 Cor. 15:24–28), it is also an expression of the ontological relationship of preincarnate, submissive Sonship (cf., e.g., John 5:18–23, 30).

The ontological relationship analogous to that between man and woman, writes Paul, is that between Father and Son (1 Cor. 11:3). That Christ submits as Son and as incarnate—that is, because of certain ontological aspects—does not mean that He is therefore inferior to the Father, nor does it cast into doubt His deity. Likewise, that the woman submits as woman does not mean that she is inferior or that her humanity as an image-bearer is threatened. In both cases, it is equals in relationship to one another. In both cases, one, because of His or her "ontological" and ordained role in relation to the other, acknowledges headship and submits. Just as no inferiority may be asserted or assumed for Christ in His submission, so also no inferiority may be asserted or assumed for woman, and no objection may be justly made because her submission rests on her cocreated identity as woman in relation to man.

"SOME OF PAUL'S TEACHING ON THIS SUBJECT, INCLUDING HIS EXEGESIS OF GENESIS 2, REFLECTS HIS RABBINIC TRAINING AND IS WRONG; IT IS AN ERRONEOUS HUMAN STATEMENT THAT SHOULD NOT BE FOLLOWED."

Jewett takes this position in a most striking and vigorous way. The full impact of this evaluation must be reckoned with. It is saying that a portion of Scripture, the Word of God, is wrong in what it professes to teach. It is saying that not only the apostle Paul but also the apostle Peter are wrong. In fact, it is saying that all the instruction we get on the subject of marriage relative to this point, and on woman in authority in the church, in the whole New Testament and even in the whole Bible, is wrong. Let that come into focus: According to this position, God has allowed His church, both in Old and New Testament days, and His apostles and writers, to communicate that which is in error and out of accord with His revealed will. And not only that: we must say also that Jesus made no attempt to correct this misunderstanding in the areas of marriage and the church. In fact, by selecting twelve *men,* Jesus perpetuated this supposedly horrendous, male-chauvinist approach.

The view that the apostles taught error is maintained over against the apostles' assertion that what they taught is God's will and is founded on God's order. Paul asserts in 1 Timothy 2 that the exclusion of women from the ruling-teaching function of the church is based on the creation order, the most basic factor that touches all people everywhere. In 1 Corinthians 11, Paul appeals to the authority relationships that God has established between the Father and the Son, the Son and man, and man and woman (v. 3); that is indeed a comprehensive appeal to interpersonal relationships, involving even the relationship of the Son and the Father. And in 1 Corinthians 11:16, he affirms that his view is the uniform view of the churches of God. In 1 Corinthians 14:34, he emphatically says that what he teaches is based on the law, another appeal to the creation order but now expressed by the term *law* as God's absolute standard. And finally, in reference to his teaching in 1 Corinthians 14–including that teaching on the subject under discussion–he says, "The things which I write to you are the Lord's commandment" (v. 37). The apostle Paul and also the apostle Peter insist the exact opposite of Jewett, and they are saying, "Thus says the Lord."

Notice finally that both the apostles and the church have realized that equality and differences of roles do indeed fit together, just as they have recognized that people are both equally image-bearers as men and women and also different as men and women. Must we view the two factors of equality and role differences as contradictory when they exist together in the creative activity of the Godhead and both express God's will?

THE BIBLICAL ATTITUDE

We must not conclude our discussion of the role relationship of men and women without also discussing the attitudes and interpersonal relationships that must exist within the structure God has ordered. The Bible, as vigorously as it establishes order in civil government, the church, and the family, always joins to its statements about authority and submission the keynote of right attitude. Once it has established the authority structure or pattern, it usually warns those in authority against misusing that authority (cf. elders in the church [1 Pet. 5:3] and fathers in the home [Eph. 6:4; Col. 3:21]). The same keynote must also be sounded in the role relationship that God has established between man and woman.

The backdrop for this affirmation is the corrosive effect of sin on interpersonal relationships in general and on that between a husband and wife in particular. It is noteworthy that Genesis 3 indicates that sin not only alienates human beings from God, but also alienates men and women (Gen. 3:16). Sin accounts for much of the hostility and antagonism between the sexes now; men and women either misuse or rebel against their particular role in relation to one another in marriage and the church. The New Testament description of one's responsibilities and obligations in marriage takes sin into account and stresses love, honor, and respect.

Thus, although the New Testament description of marriage affirms vigorously the husband-wife relationship as that of head and helper, it asks each partner to do what he or she is least likely to do (Eph. 5:22ff.; Col. 3:18-19; 1 Pet. 3:1-7). To the husband as authority figure comes the vigorous admonition to love (as Christ loves the church), not to be bitter, and to honor his wife. To the wife as the under-authority figure comes the vigorous admonition to respect her husband and to submit ("as to the Lord" and as the church submits to Christ) "in everything." The tendency for the one in authority, affected by sin, is to be callous and overweening, disregarding the person and feelings of the one under his authority; but the New Testament requires just the opposite of husbands: "Live with your wives in an understanding way, as with a weaker vessel, since she is a woman; and grant her honor as a fellow-heir of the grace of life, so that your prayers may not be hindered" (1 Pet. 3:7). The tendency for one under authority, affected by sin, is to be sullen and disrespectful, complying as little as possible; but the New Testament requires just the opposite of the wife: "Let the wife see to it that she respect her husband" (Eph. 5:33; cf. 5:22–23; 1 Pet. 3:4, 6).

But even those words and truths must be set in their wider context, and that context is the mutual submission that all Christians–men and women, husbands and wives–must render to each other under the headship of and in respect for the Lord Jesus Christ (Eph. 5:21: "Be subject to one another in the fear of Christ"; cf. 1 Cor. 11:11–12: "However, in the Lord, neither is woman independent of man, nor is man independent of woman"). The basis for all proper role relationships is that we all belong to, need, and must submit to one another as joint-heirs of the grace of life. Even in exercising his function as leader of others in the church, an elder or bishop must serve others. Even in exercising his headship over his wife, the husband must submit to and honor her as a joint heir of the grace of life, an equal by both creation and redemption (again cf. 1 Pet. 3:7). Elders and husbands are heads not because they are inherently superior—for they exercise their functions among and with equals—but because they have been called by God to their tasks.

It is that combined keynote of submission and equality in exercising leadership that I fear has been lost not only in the secular women's liberation movement, but also on the part of the more strident voices within the Christian community. And to do so is to fall into the infighting for the places of honor and authority that the disciples of Jesus did (cf. Matt. 20:20–28 and parallels). (Parenthetically, Jesus' concept of servanthood renders groundless the charge that an appeal to submission is but an echo of authoritarianism and an "opiate for the people.") In His reply to His disciples, Jesus does not deny that some are called to positions of leadership; He does attempt to deal with the root sin of pride, arrogance, and self-righteousness. The model for all Christians, and especially for those in positions of leadership or headship, is Jesus Himself: "You know that the rulers of the Gentiles lord it over them, and their great men exercise authority over them. It is not so among you, but whoever wishes to become great among you shall be your servant, and whoever wishes to be first among you shall be your slave; just as the Son of Man did not come to be served, but to serve, and to give His life a ransom for many" (Matt. 20:25–28).

The Christian church and individual Christians will most likely face in the coming day the charge that they are unrighteous and unjust in denying to women leadership roles in marriage and the church, or at least in not abolishing male leadership roles. We may well be maligned as unprincipled or prejudiced people, and we may suffer economic and legal sanctions. In such times when God's unchanging Word clashes with man's changing culture, let us fortify ourselves with the truth that

> All flesh is like grass,
> And all its glory like the flower of grass.
> The grass withers,
> And the flower falls off,
> But the word of the Lord abides forever.
>
> (1 Pet. 1:24–25)

Appendix 1:
Does *kephalē* ("head") Mean "Source" or "Authority Over" in Greek Literature?
A Survey of 2,336 Examples

Wayne Grudem

When the New Testament says that the "head of every man is Christ" and "the head of a woman is the man" (1 Cor. 11:3), or that "the husband is the head of the wife as Christ is the head of the church" (Eph. 5:23), Christians have usually understood the word *head* to mean "authority over." Thus, Christ is the authority over the church and a husband is the authority over his wife.

But that information has been challenged recently by those who claim, at least for some passages, that the word *head* means "source" or "origin" rather than "authority over." Thus, Christ is the *source* of every man, Christ is the *source* of the church, and—referring to Adam and Eve—the man is the *source* of the woman. It is the purpose of this appendix to examine that recent claim on the basis of a survey of more than 2,300 examples of the Greek word *kephalē* ("head") from ancient Greek literature.

ARGUMENTS IN FAVOR OF THE MEANING "SOURCE"

MODERN AUTHORS

Perhaps the most influential and explicit statement of the position that *kephalē* means "source" was the article, "Does Male

Dominance Tarnish Our Translations?" by Berkeley and Alvera Mickelsen. The Mickelsens argued that *head* in Greek usage "does not mean 'boss' or 'final authority,'" but that a "common meaning" was "source, or origin, as we use it in the 'head of the Mississippi River'" (p. 23). They suggested the meaning "source" for the word *head* in 1 Corinthians 11:3 and Colossians 1:18.[1]

Other writers make similar claims. Regarding 1 Corinthians 11:3, Margaret Howe states, "The word *head* here must be understood not as 'ruler' but as 'source.' Christ came from God; he is 'the only Son from the Father' (John 1:14). As the agent of creation (John 1:3), Christ brought the man into being ... and from the male of the species, the female came into being (Gen. 2:21–22)."[2]

Letha Scanzoni and Nancy Hardesty say, "*Kephalē* is used almost synonomously with *archē*, 'beginning,' somewhat similar to our use of 'the headwaters of a river' or 'fountain head.'" Thus, when Ephesians 5:23 says "Christ is the head of the church, his body," they take it to mean that He is the church's "lifegiver." And when Colossians 2:10 calls Christ "the head of all rule and authority," Scanzoni and Hardesty say, "'Head' here obviously means 'source.'" Similarly, "Christ's headship over the church refers to his being the source of its life."[3]

Richard and Joyce Boldrey apparently support this interpretation when they say of 1 Corinthians 11, "When Paul spoke of woman's head being the man, he was emphasizing man's temporal priority and woman's derivation from him."[4]

The foregoing authors represent what we may call a "Christian feminist" perspective; others who do not generally endorse

1. Berkeley Mickelsen and Alvera Mickelsen, "Does Male Dominance Tarnish Our Translations?" *Christianity Today*, 5 October 1979, pp. 23–29. (See also their article, "The 'Head' of the Epistles," *Christianity Today*, 20 February 1931, pp. 20–23.)
2. Margaret Howe, *Women and Church Leadership* (Grand Rapids: Zondervan, 1982), p. 60.
3. Letha Scanzoni and Nancy Hardesty, *All We're Meant to Be* (Waco, Tex.: Word, 1974), pp. 30–31; 100.
4. Richard Boldrey and Joyce Boldrey, *Chauvinist or Feminist? Paul's View of Women* (Grand Rapids: Baker, 1976), p. 34.

the Christian feminist position have also supported this view of *kephalē*. Commenting on 1 Corinthians 11:3, F. F. Bruce writes, "By *head* in this context we are probably to understand not, as has frequently been suggested, 'chief' or 'ruler' but rather 'source' or 'origin'—a sense well attested for Greek *kephalē*." Similarly, C. K. Barrett says, "In Greek usage the word, when metaphorical, may apply ... to origin.... That this is the sense of the word here is strongly suggested by verses 8f." Colin Brown says of 1 Corinthians 11:3, "Here 'head' is probably to be understood not as 'chief' or 'ruler' but as 'source,' or 'origin.'" And James Hurley, although retaining the sense "authority over" in 1 Corinthians 11:3, allows the meaning "source" in Colossians 2:19 and Ephesians 4:15. He says, "In English we speak of the 'head' of a river to refer to its point of origin. This was a typical usage of 'head' (*kephalē*) in classical Greek.... In Paul's day, therefore, the Greek word 'head' (*kephalē*) could mean a physical head, a person with authority, or the source of something. Head (*kephalē*) was used in first-century Greek as a synonym for the more common words for 'ruler' (*archōn*) and for 'source' (*archē*)."[5]

SUMMARY OF EVIDENCE SUPPORTING THE MEANING "SOURCE"

The repeated claim by these authors is that *source* was a commonly known or easily recognized sense of the word *head* (*kephalē*) for the Greek-speaking readers of Paul's epistles. Indeed, that point must be established by anyone arguing for the meaning "source" in the New Testament. For if we cannot show that "source" was a recognized meaning of *kephalē* in the ancient world, then we must conclude that no such possible meaning would have come to the minds of Paul or his readers, and we

5. F. F. Bruce, *1 and 2 Corinthians* (London: Marshall, Morgan and Scott, 1971), p. 103; C. K. Barrett, *The First Epistle to the Corinthians* (London: Black, 1971), p. 248; Colin Brown, "Head," in *New International Dictionary of New Testament Theology* (Grand Rapids: Zondervan, 1976) 2:156–63; James Hurley, *Man and Woman in Biblical Perspective* (London: Inter-Varsity, 1981), p. 164.

shall be forced to look at other possible senses to interpret the New Testament passages in question.

What kind of evidence is needed? The same kind needed to establish the possible meaning of any word in ancient literature: brief quotations from a few occurrences of the word in any ancient Greek writer where the context makes it clear that the author is using *kephalē* to mean "source." That is the common procedure for establishing possible meanings for words in all New Testament study; if "source" is to be considered a legitimate sense of *kephalē*, we must have such evidence.

The need for such clear examples becomes even more important because "source" is not listed as a possible meaning for *kephalē* in the standard lexicon for New Testament Greek by Bauer, Arndt, Gingrich, and Danker. Nor do the older New Testament lexicons by Thayer or Cremer list such a sense; nor does the lexicon to the papyri by Moulton and Milligan.[6] (See the discussion below regarding the entry in Liddell-Scott, the lexicon for classical—not specifically New Testament—Greek.)

Thus authors who propose the sense "source" are proposing a new meaning, one previously unrecognized by New Testament lexicons. That does not make the meaning "source" impossible, but it does mean that we are right to demand some convincing citations from ancient Greek literature that the editors of these lexicons had overlooked or misunderstood.

The evidence given by the previously mentioned authors is as follows: Margaret Howe, Richard and Joyce Boldrey, and Letha Scanzoni and Nancy Hardesty cite no evidence from ancient literature or from other scholars. F. F. Bruce and James Hurley cite no evidence from ancient literature, but both refer to an

6. W. Bauer, W. F. Arndt, F. W. Gingrich, and F. W. Danker, *A Greek-English Lexicon of the New Testament and Other Early Christian Literature*, 2d ed. rev. (Chicago: U. of Chicago, 1979); Joseph H. Thayer, *Greek-English Lexicon of the New Testament* (Grand Rapids: Zondervan, 1956; Hermann Cremer, *Biblico-Theological Lexicon of New Testament Greek*, trans. W. Urwick (1886; reprint, Naperville, Ill.: Allenson, n.d.); J. H. Moulton and G. Milligan, *The Vocabulary of the Greek Testament: Illustrated From the Papyri and Other Non-Literary Sources*, 2 vols. (New York: Gordon, 1977).

article by Stephen Bedale.[7] Hurley says that Bedale "provides careful documentation of the meaning of *kephalē*" (p. 164, n. 1). Colin Brown cites no evidence from ancient literature but refers to the commentary by F. F. Bruce and the article by Bedale. Berkeley and Alvera Mickelsen cite no evidence from ancient literature, but they do refer to the meaning "source" listed in the Liddell-Scott lexicon for classical Greek. The entry in this Liddell-Scott lexicon cites Herodotus 4.91 and *Orphic Fragments* 21a as evidence for the meaning "source."[8] C. K. Barrett also mentions the Bedale article and cites Herodotus 4.91 (correctly noting that the plural "heads" is used there) and *Orphic Fragments* 21a, the same two texts cited by the Liddell-Scott lexicon. Thus, apart from the "careful documentation" we have been told to expect in the article by Bedale, the actual hard data adduced to support the meaning "source" turn out to consist of just two texts.

Moreover, upon reading the frequently-cited article by Bedale we are surprised to find that he does not cite even one text from ancient Greek literature outside the Bible. Thus the widely accepted argument for a "common" use of *kephalē* to mean "source" in extra-Biblical Greek literature has rested on only two occurrences of the word. Whether or not those will actually support the argument must be decided by looking at the two texts themselves. But before we do that, it is appropriate to analyze briefly the 1954 article by Bedale.

THE ARGUMENT BY BEDALE

Bedale bases his argument for the meaning "source" in 1 Corinthians 11:3, Ephesians 4:15, and Colossians 2:19 on the following three points:

(1) Kephalē *does not normally mean "ruler."* Bedale says, "In normal Greek usage, classical or contemporary, *kephalē* does not

7. Stephen Bedale, "The Meaning of *kephalē* in the Pauline Epistles, *Journal of Theological Studies* 5 (1954): 211–15.
8. H. G. Liddell and Robert Scott, eds., *A Greek–English Lexicon*, 9th ed., with Supplement (Oxford: Clarendon, 1968).

signify 'head' in the sense of ruler, or chieftan, of a community."[9] Bedale cites no evidence—no results of word studies, no lexical authorities—to demonstrate his point; he simply assumes it to be true for the rest of the article.

In the following major section of this essay I will quote thirty-two examples of *kephalē* used to mean "authority over" or "ruler" in Greek writings outside the New Testament (seventeen are from Greek translations of the Old Testament and fifteen are from other literature). On the basis of those quotations it is safe to conclude that this first point of Bedale's argument is simply a misstatement of the facts and cannot be accepted as valid.

(2) The ancient world did not think that the head controlled the body. Bedale's second point of support is the assertion that Paul and his readers would not think of the head as the ruling or controlling part of the body, for that idea was contrary to popular psychology in the ancient world. In fact, Bedale says that J. Armitage Robinson is "guilty of serious anachronism" (p. 212) when Robinson writes that it is natural to think of Christ as the body's head in Ephesians 4:15, "for," says Robinson, "that is the seat of the brain which controls and unifies the organism." Bedale says that such a metaphor "would be unintelligible to St. Paul or his readers.... In St. Paul's day, according to popular psychology, both Greek and Hebrew, a man reasoned and purposed, not 'with his head,' but 'in his heart'"[10]

Is Bedale correct in asserting that the ancient world did not think of the head as controlling or ruling the body? Once again he gives no evidence to support this affirmation. In fact, there is significant evidence to contradict it. Plato (5th–4th cent. B.C.), describing the parts of the human body, wrote of "the head which is the most divine part and which reigns (*despoteō*) over all the parts within us" (*Timaeus* 44.D). Plutarch (A.D. 46–120), one of the most prominent Greek authors from the New Testament

9. Bedale, p. 211.
10. Ibid., p. 212.

period (and, one who reflected secular thinking independent of Jewish or Christian influence), explained why the words *soul* (*psychē*) and *head* (*kephalē*) can be used to speak of the whole person: "We affectionately call a person 'soul' or 'head' from his ruling parts (*apo tōn kuriotatōn*)" (*Table-Talk* 692.D.11). Philo (Jewish philosopher, c. 30 B.C.—c. A.D. 45), representing one aspect of first century Judaism, had a similar understanding: "As the head in the living body is the ruling place (*to hēgemoneuon tropon*), so Ptolemy became head among kings" (*Life of Moses* 2.30). "The mind is the head and ruler (*hēgemonikon*) of the sense-perception in us" (*Life of Moses* 2.82); "'Head' we interpret allegorically to be the ruling (*hēgemona*) mind of the soul" (*On Dreams* 2.207).

In light of those statements from three very diverse authors, Bedale's second major point, that a metaphor of the head ruling the body "would be unintelligible to St. Paul or his readers," must be rejected as contrary to fact and therefore invalid.

(3) The Septuagint shows that kephalē *can mean "source."* This is Bedale's final major point. He argues as follows:

(a) The Hebrew word *ro'sh* ("head") was translated sometimes by *kephalē* and sometimes by *archē* ("beginning" or "ruler") in the Septuagint (the Greek translation of the Old Testament used by both Jews and Christians in the first century). (b) When *ro'sh* meant a literal head of a person or animal, or the "top" of some object, the Septuagint translated it with *kephalē*. (c) When *ro'sh* meant "first" or "beginning"—as it sometimes did in the Hebrew Old Testament—it was translated by *archē*. (d) When *ro'sh* meant "ruler" or "chief" it was translated by either *kephalē* or *archē* (even though more often than either of those it was translated by *archōn* or *archēgos*, more common words for "ruler"). (This point, incidentally, admits the meaning of "ruler" for Septuagint Greek and thus seems to contradict Bedale's first major argument—unless he means to exclude the Septuagint by using the phrase "normal Greek usage." (e) Consequently, "in St. Paul's usage, *kephalē* may very well approximate in meaning to *arche*." (f) Bedale concludes that since *archē* sometimes means "source," *kephalē* in Paul's writings may mean "source" as well, and he applies this to 1 Corinthians 11:3, Ephesians 4:15, and Colossians 2:19."[11]

How should this third argument be evaluated? It is a classic example of a major exegetical error. Bedale has skipped from the idea that in one sense ("ruler") *kephalē* and *archē* have the same meaning (point *d* above) to an unwarranted assertion that in *other* senses ("beginning," "source"), or perhaps in *all* senses, they have the same meaning (points *e* and *f* above). He even speaks of a "virtual equation of *kephalē* with *archē*."[12] But he gives not one text to demonstrate that the words share the meanings "source" or "beginning."

In fact, the reader will search Bedale's article in vain for any examples showing that *kephalē* ever meant "source" in the Septuagint. It is understandable that *archē*, which sometimes meant "leader," would be interchangeable with *kephalē* in Old Testament texts in which the concept "ruler" is present. But that fact alone does not demonstrate that *kephalē* could take on other senses of *archē* such as "source."

A parallel to Bedale's argument in English would be if I were to argue (1) that "jump" and "spring" could both be used to translate some foreign word when it referred to a "leap in the air," and (2) that therefore there is a "virtual equation of 'jump' and 'spring' in English." I would then go on to argue that "jump" *also* can mean "a fountain of water," or "a coil of metal," or "a pleasant season of the year when flowers begin to bloom." If I produced no unambiguous examples of written texts where "jump" clearly took these senses, readers would rightly think my reasoning erroneous and invalid.

Similarly, since Bedale has produced no example of Septuagint texts in which *kephalē* means "source," his third and final argument must be rejected as faulty in reasoning, unsupported by any hard facts, and therefore invalid. We may hope that Bedale's article will no longer be quoted as proving that *kephalē* at the time of the New Testament could mean "source," for his

11. Ibid., p. 213.
12. Ibid.

first two points are simply contrary to fact, and his third point commits a major exegetical blunder that leads him to a false conclusion.

If Bedale's article does not prove that *kephalē* can mean "source," we are left with only two remaining pieces of evidence that have been used to prove that meaning: Herodotus 4.91 and *Orphic Fragments* 21a.

THE EVIDENCE FROM ANCIENT LITERATURE

Herodotus (5th cent. B.C.) says, "From the heads (*kephalai*, plural) of the Tearus River flows water most pleasant and good" (4.91). But when we look again at the Liddell-Scott lexicon under *kephalē*, we find that *kephalē* refers to the source of a river only in the plural; in the singular it means "mouth" of a river (they cite Callimachus, *Aetia* 2.46, "I know Gela [a city], placed at the mouth [*kephalē*] of a river," referring to Gela on the south coast of Sicily at the mouth of the Gelas River).

How can the same word refer to the sources of a river in the plural, but the mouth of the river in the singular? The answer is evident from an examination of the general category of meanings listed under this sense (II) in Liddell-Scott: "of things, extremity." That is, the end point or furthest extension of an item can be called its *head:* the "top, brim of a vessel"; the "capital of a column"; the "coping of a wall"; the "head of a garlic"; the "base of the heart"; the "origin [in the sense of "point of origin" or "starting point"] of muscles"; the "extremity of a plot of land"; the "beginning of a period of time." (They give examples for all of these.) We see this sense of "end point" in Psalm 118:22 (LXX Ps. 117:22), "The stone which the builders rejected has become the head (*kephalē*) of the corner," namely, the starting point or furthest end stone of the corner. (That verse is quoted in Matt. 21:42; Mk. 12:10; Lk. 20:17; Acts 4:11; and 1 Pet. 2:7, all using *kephalē*.) In fact, *kephalē* takes the sense "top" or "end point" 22 times in the Septuagint alone. (Gen. 8:5; 11:14; 28:12; 2 Chr. 3:16; Job 1:17, et al). For example, the ends of the poles used to carry the Ark of the Covenant are called the "heads" of the poles in the Septuagint translation of 1 Kings 8:8 (LXX 3 Kings 8:8). This is a natural and understandable extension of the word *head*, since our heads are at the "top" or "end" of our bodies.

Now the river quotations become clear. Someone speaking of the "heads" of a river is speaking of the many "ends" of a river where tributaries begin to flow toward the main stream. On the other hand, someone speaking of the "head" of a river is speaking of the one point at which the river enters into the sea, what we call in English the "mouth" of the river. Therefore these examples from Herodotus and elsewhere do not prove a new meaning ("source") for *kephalē*, but only provide specific examples of a well-established and long-recognized sense, "top, furthest extension, end point, beginning point." Indeed, that is exactly what the editors of Liddell-Scott intended, for they placed the river examples as a subcategory under general category II, "of things, extremity."

Those who cite Herodotus or the "head of a river" examples to show that *kephalē* could have meant "source" at the time of the New Testament have not been careful enough in their use of Herodotus or Liddell-Scott. First, it is improper to take a meaning from a category that is specifically stated to apply to "things" and then apply it to persons. Second, when Liddell-Scott specifies that the plural refers to a river's "source" whereas the singular applies to the river's "mouth," it is improper to use the meaning that applies only to the *plural* ("source") for the instances in the New Testament, all of which are *singular*. If one insists on applying the river quotations to the husband-wife statements in the New Testament, for example, he will have to use the singular sense and obtain the meaning, "the husband is the mouth of the wife." The absurdity of that sentence is evident at once, but in terms of use of the Liddell-Scott lexicon it is based on exactly the same procedure as those who claim "source of a river" to prove that *kephalē* means "source" in the New Testament. (Indeed, the procedure is in a formal way one degree more valid, because it at least uses a singular sense to define a singular New Testament noun.)

We conclude that Herodotus 4.19 shows that the plural of *kephalē* can refer to the "end points" or "extremities" of a thing, and that this text therefore cannot be validly used to show that *kephalē* meant "source" generally at the time of the New Testament.

That leaves only one text, *Orphic Fragments* 21a, to prove that "source" was a "common meaning" at the time of the New Testament.[13] The *Orphic Fragments* are a collection of fragments of poems preserved from a very early date in Greek literature. Of these fragments the *Oxford Classical Dictionary* states, "The dates and personalities of the alleged authors are unknown to us."[14] Because Plato (c. 429–347 B.C.) quotes from them, they cannot be dated later than the fifth century B.C. That does not make them completely invalid as evidence for the possible meaning of a word at the time of the New Testament; but it must be said that only one example of a word used in a fragmentary poem by an unknown author of unknown date 500 or more years before the time of the New Testament is probably the weakest possible evidence that one could imagine. I know of no other case in which a common New Testament word has been endowed with a new meaning on the basis of such evidence, and readers might well be forgiven for suspecting that an argument constructed on such a slim basis would be guilty of special pleading. But let us examine the text nonetheless.[15]

The translation of the text is:

13. Mickelsen and Mickelsen, p. 23.
14. N. G. L. Hammond and H. H. Scullard, eds., *Oxford Classical Dictionary*, 2d ed. (Oxford: Clarendon, 1970), p. 759.
15. The critical edition of the text is found in Otto Kern, *Orphicorum Fragmenta* (Berlin: Weidmannsche Verlagsbüchhandlung, 1922), p. 91. It reads:

     Ζεὺς πρῶτος γένετο, Ζεὺς ὕστατος ἀργικέραυνος·
     Ζεὺς κεφαλή, Ζεὺς μέσσα· Διὸς δ᾽ ἐκ πάντα τελεῖται

     The text is quoted in Aristotle, *On the Cosmos* 7 (401a.29–30), found in vol. 3, p. 406 of the Loeb Classical Library edition of Aristotle, and may be conveniently consulted there by the reader without access to Kern's critical text. The Loeb text has *archikeraunos*, "ruler of lightning," as a variant reading in the first line and *tetuktai* instead of *teleitai* in the second line.

Zeus was first, Zeus is last with white, vivid lightning:
Zeus the head, Zeus the middle, Zeus from whom all things
    are perfected.

Both the critical text by Kern and the Liddell-Scott lexicon note that the word *kephalē* is not established with certainty as the correct reading here, because another copy of the text has *archē*, "beginning," instead of *kephalē*, "head." Thus, this bit of evidence is somewhat weaker still: it is just one of two possible variant readings.

Nevertheless, what does *kephalē* mean in this text? Even if "source" were a well-attested meaning of *kephalē* in many other texts, it is doubtful that "source" would be the best meaning here. The sense "beginning" (of a series) or "first one" (in terms of time) seems most likely here because of (1) the similarity to the idea of "first" and "last" in the previous line and (2) the contrast with "middle" and the mention of perfection in the same line— giving the sense, "Zeus is the beginning, Zeus is the middle, Zeus is the one who completes all things." The variant reading *archē*, which can mean "beginning" as well as "source" (or "ruler") would also fit that sense well. Now that is not to say that the writer of this poetry was denying that all things come from Zeus or that Zeus is the origin of all things. Indeed, subsequent lines affirm things close to that idea. I am simply arguing that the context shows that the author is not talking about whether Zeus or someone or something else is the source or origin of all things; he is rather affirming that in terms of time Zeus was first and Zeus will be last as well. (For example, my oldest son is the "beginning" or "first" of my sons, but he is not the "source" of my other sons.)

Thus, even if *kephalē* could be shown from other texts sometimes to take the meaning "source," it would seem an inappropriate sense in this text. And because no other examples of *kephalē* meaning "source" are given by Liddell-Scott or cited by other authors, it seems that the meaning "source" should be ruled out as even a possibility in this text as well.

Regarding the entry in the Liddell-Scott lexicon, which

quotes *Orphic Fragments* 21a as the only evidence for the general meaning "source, origin," it would be more accurate if the entry were classified under the category "starting-point." Indeed, that would allow the entry to fit more easily under the general category in which the editors have placed it, "of things, extremity," for in this case the thing referred to is a period of time.

Thus, even this obscure support for the meaning "source" fails to be legitimate, and we are left with no evidence to convince us that "source" was a common or even a possible meaning for *kephalē* in Greek literature. Those who claim that *kephalē* could mean "source" at the time of the New Testament should be aware that the claim has so far been supported by not one clear instance in all of Greek literature, and it is therefore a claim made without any real factual support. The editors of the standard lexicons for New Testament Greek (such as Bauer-Arndt-Gingrich-Danker) have been correct not to include "source" among their lists of possible meanings for *kephalē*.

CAN KEPHALĒ MEAN "AUTHORITY OVER"?

Even if *kephalē* did not mean "source" at the time of the New Testament, are we correct in understanding it to mean "authority over"? When we read that "Christ is the head of the church" or that "the husband is the head of the wife" (Eph. 5:23), are we right to think that it means Christ is the "authority over" the church and the husband is the "authority over" his wife?

THE MICKELSENS' ARGUMENT

Some authors have denied that "authority over" was a legitimate sense of *kephalē* at the time of the New Testament. Berkeley and Alvera Mickelsen, for example, claim "that 'head' in Greek usage (according to the standard Greek-English Lexicon by Liddell, Scott, Jones, McKenzie) does *not* mean 'boss' or 'final authority.'" They say, "For Greek-speaking people in New Testament times who had little opportunity to read the Greek translation of the Old Testment, there were many possible meanings for 'head' but 'supreme over' or 'being responsible to' were not among them."[16]

The evidence the Mickelsens give to support the claim that *kephalē* did not mean "authority over" is that the meaning is not listed in the Liddell-Scott lexicon. But one wonders why the Mickelsens cited only that lexicon and no others. In fact, Liddell-Scott is the standard lexicon for all of Greek literature from about 700 B.C. to about A.D. 600 with emphasis on classical Greek authors in the seven centuries prior to the New Testament. Liddell-Scott is the tool one would use when studying Plato or Aristotle, for example; but it is not the standard lexicon that scholars use for the study of the New Testament. (The standard lexicon for that is Bauer-Arndt-Gingrich-Danker, which the Mickelsens fail to mention in their article.) Although the Liddell-Scott lexicon usually does list examples of meanings from both the New Testament and the Septuagint, its treatment of those areas is necessarily very limited; it is not nearly as detailed in those areas as the Bauer-Arndt-Gingrich-Danker lexicon. So the absence of a certain sense of *kephalē* from Liddell-Scott is certainly not conclusive evidence for deciding whether *kephalē* can in fact take that sense.[17]

16. Mickelsen and Mickelsen, pp. 23, 25.
17. In their subsequent article, "The 'Head' of the Epistles" (*Christianity Today*, 20 February 1981, pp. 20–23), the Mickelsens argue that *kephalē* only infrequently meant "ruler, authority" in the Septuagint (seventeen times), and that *archōn*, "ruler," was much more commonly used to mean "ruler, authority," when translating the Hebrew word for "head" (*ro'sh*). But that argument simply proves that *kephalē* is less common than *archōn* in this sense, not that it could not take this sense. (In fact, the seventeen LXX instances prove that it could.)

In this article they also discuss the Bauer-Arndt-Gingrich-Danker lexicon, but they argue that it wrongfully allows the meaning "ruler, authority" (more precisely, "in the case of living beings, to denote superior rank," p. 430) in the New Testament. They suggest (pp. 21–22) not only the meaning "source" but also several other possible meanings in the relevant New Testament passages: "exalted originator and completor" (for Col. 1:18), "nourisher" (for Eph. 4:15 and Col. 2:10), "base" or "derivation" (for 1 Cor. 11:3), and "enabler" (for Eph. 5:23 and Col. 2:10). What they fail to mention is that not one of these new meanings they suggest is

THE EVIDENCE FROM NEW TESTAMENT GREEK LEXICONS

In fact, all the standard lexicons and dictionaries for New Testament Greek do list the meaning "authority over" for *kephalē,* "head." Bauer-Arndt-Gingrich-Danker give under the word *kephalē* the following definition: "In the case of living beings, to denote superior rank." They list thirteen examples of such usage.

The article on *kephalē* in the *Theological Dictionary of the New Testament,* in examining the use of *kephalē* in the Septuagint, says, "*kephalē* is used for the head or ruler of a society." The author (Heinrich Schlier) cites several examples.[18]

In *The New International Dictionary of New Testament Theology,* volume 2, in the article "Head," K. Munzer says that the relationship of head to body in Colossians 2:10 "expresses the authority of Christ . . . and the corresponding subordination of the church" (p. 162).

The older New Testament lexicons by Thayer and Cremer give similar statements. Thayer's lexicon says under *kephalē,* "Metaphorically anything *supreme, chief, prominent;* of persons, *master, lord* "; it lists several examples.

---

found in any Greek lexicon—Liddell-Scott, Bauer-Arndt-Gingrich-Danker, or any other. Thus they have gone beyond the previous mistake of a wrong use of the meaning "source" from Liddell-Scott (see above, p. 51) and created several additional meanings somewhat loosely related to the English word *source,* meanings that have no lexical support whatever. Yet they call these new meanings "common Greek meanings" (p. 21) and "recognized Greek meanings that would have been familiar to his [Paul's] readers" (p. 23). Such statements must be rejected for lack of any clear factual support—they are simply false.

18. Gerhard Kittel and Gerhard Friedrich, eds., *Theological Dictionary of the New Testament,* 10 vols. (Grand Rapids: Eerdmans, 1964–76) 3:673–82. Schlier does not deny the sense "authority over" for the New Testament, but his analysis of the New Testament material is heavily biased by his assumption that we have in the New Testament "both the ideas and terminology of the Gnostic myth" (p. 681). In the New Testament, he says, "We are in the sphere of the Gnostic redeemer myth" (p. 680). Thus, he interprets many of the New Testament references in terms of later Gnostic mythology, a procedure that would be followed by few scholars and probably no evangelicals today.

Cremer, under *kephalē* says, "The head is that part of the body which holds together and governs all the outgoings of life ... and because of its vital connection stands in the relation of ruler to the other members." Cremer cites Colossians 1:18; 2:19; 1 Corinthians 11:3; Ephesians 1:22; 4:15–16; and 5:23 in this connection.

Because all those widely recognized reference tools for New Testament Greek affirm the sense "authority over" for *kephalē*, one finds it hard to accept the claim of the Mickelsens that *kephalē* could not mean "authority over" in ordinary Greek at the time of the New Testament.

A SURVEY OF 2,336 EXAMPLES

But what is the actual evidence from ancient Greek literature? Are there texts that clearly use *kephalē* in the meaning "authority over"? If so, is it a frequent meaning and one that would have been understandable to readers of the New Testament epistles?

Instead of examining only the examples listed in lexicons, I decided to conduct a more extensive survey of the use of *kephalē* in ancient Greek literature. Such a survey has recently become feasible on a scale never before possible because of the existence of the Thesaurus Linguae Graecae (TLG) project at the University of California-Irvine. This project, which is still in process, currently has more than 20 million words from ancient Greek texts on a computerized database. When I inquired about *kephalē*, the TLG people informed me that a quick check showed about 12,000 instances of *kephalē* in their database. That was so large a list that it would have been practically impossible to check them all. I decided instead to check all the instances of *kephalē* in the authors included in the TLG's "Basic Text Package, tape A." This includes almost all the authors of major importance for classical Greek, and several others as well. This set of authors gave me about 2,000 usable instances of *kephalē* dating from the eighth century B.C. (Homer) onward, and ranging over all sorts of literature, including history, philosophy, drama, poetry, rhetoric, geography, and romantic writings. It provided an excellent and, it seems to me, unbiased selection of the instances of *kephalē*. I looked up every instance available to me and included them all in the following summary.[19]

To the TLG package I added all the instances of *kephalē* in the following authors: Philo, Josephus, the Apostolic Fathers, the Epistle of Aristeas, the Testaments of the Twelve Patriarchs, and Aquila, Symmachus, and Theodotian. That gave me 323 additional instances of *kephalē* that were much closer to the time and language of the New Testament than the majority of the other authors in the TLG package.

The result was a survey of 2,336 instances of *kephalē* in 36 authors from the eighth century B.C. to the fourth century A.D. In each case listed below, all the extant writings of an author were searched and every instance of *kephalē* was examined and tabulated with the exception of fragmentary texts and a few other minor works that were unavailable to me. The edition used was the Loeb Classical Library edition where available; otherwise, standard texts and translations were used.[20]

19. I am extremely grateful to my teaching assistant, Thomas Locheed, for checking all the instances in Aristotle for me, and to a former teaching assistant, Morris Johnson, for doing an initial survey of all the instances in Philo, Josephus, the Septuagint, and some minor Christian and Jewish writings. I am also grateful for the kind assistance of the TLG staff, and especially Research Assistant Ms. Virginia Anastasopoulos, in providing me with the necesary data for this survey.

20. To be more precise, the works of the authors listed were consulted in their entirety with the exception of the following: fragments of works from Aeschylus, Aristophanes, and Callimachus; 49 examples in *History of Animals* and some minor works and fragments by Aristotle; 7 instances in Xenophon; 6 instances in minor works of Plutarch, and many instances in the fourth-century A.D. author Libanius (only selections from his works were available in the Loeb edition, which I used). In addition, the totals represented do not count two erroneous translations in Aquila's text of Deuteronomy 29:18 and 32:33, which are of uncertain meaning. Moreover, the following authors in the basic text package, tape A, were not in the Loeb Classical Library and I did not pursue them: Chariton (10 instances), Heliodorus (44 instances), Herodas (0 instances), Nicander Colophonius (5 instances), Pseudo-Plutarch (12 instances), Xenophon of Ephesus (1 instance).

With those exceptions, all instances are included and tabulated. After

AUTHORS	NUMBER OF INSTANCES CHECKED
8th century B.C.	
Homer (poet)	141
7th century B.C.	
Hesiod (poet)	18
5th century B.C.	
Aeschylus (tragic dramatist)	1
Aristophanes (comic dramatist)	56
Euripides (dramatist)	13
Herodotus (historian)	114
Plato (5th/4th century philosopher)	97
Sophocles (dramatist)	1
Thucydides (historian)	4
4th century B.C.	
Aristotle (philosopher)	296
Demosthenes (orator)	16
Greek anthology (various authors:	
4th c. B.C. and later)	72
Xenophon (historian)	47
3d century B.C.	
Apollonius Rhodius, (poet)	13
Aratus Soleus (poet)	35
Callimachus (poet)	5
Septuagint (various translators;	
3d to 1st c. B.C.)	519
Theocritus (poet)	1
2d century B.C.	
Epistle of Aristeas	2
Testaments of the Twelve Patriarchs	10
1st century B.C.	
Parthenius Nichaenus (poet)	1
1st century A.D.	
Apostolic Fathers	16
Josephus (Jewish historian, A.D. 37–100)	125
New Testament	74
Philo (Jewish philosopher;	
flourished around A.D. 40)	120

examining over 2,300 examples, it did not seem to me that the additional work involved in chasing down those more obscure references would have any significant effect on the results of the study, so I decided not to make further efforts to obtain them.

Plutarch (secular historian and philosopher, A.D. 46–120)	277
2d century A.D.	
Achilles Tatius (romantic writer)	37
Pausanius (geographer)	98
Aquila, Symmachus, and Theodotian (translators of the Old Testament)	50
3d century A.D.	
Diogenes Laertius (biographer)	17
Longus (romantic writer)	7
4th century A.D.	
Libanius (orator)	39
	2,336

The results of this survey and tabulation of uses of *kephalē* are as follows:

Meanings	Number of instances	Percentage of total instances	Percentage of 302 metaphorical uses only (all uses except 1.a.)
1. *Of persons or other living beings*			
a. Physical head of man or animal	2,034	87	———
b. Head referred to in adverbial phrase such as "headlong," "overhead," "head downwards," etc.	28	1.2	9.3
c. "Head" used to refer to the whole person	119	5.1	39.4
d. "Head" used to mean "life" (as in capital punishment)	14	0.6	4.6
e. Person of superior authority or rank, or "ruler," "ruling part"	49	2.1	16.2
2. *Of things*			
a. Extremity, end, top; "starting point" in series or row	69	3.0	22.9
b. Prominent part	6	0.3	2.0
c. In arguments: summary, conclusion, or main point	17	0.7	5.6

3. *"Source, origin"*: person or thing from which something else is derived or obtained	0*	0	0
Totals	2,336	100	100

* As explained above, I classified Herodotus 4.91 and *Orphic Fragments* 21a under meaning 2a (see pp. 57–61).

As might be expected, the great majority of instances of *kephalē* refer to an actual physical head of a man or animal. The other uses are all metaphorical in some sense or other.

For our purposes, it is significant to note that the sense "ruler" or "person of superior authority or rank" occurs 49 times, which is 16.2 percent of the instances in which *kephalē* is used in a metaphorical sense. Of those, 12 are from the New Testament, 13 from the Septuagint, 5 from other Greek translations of the Old Testament, 2 from Herodotus, 1 from Plato, 1 from the Testaments of the Twelve Patriarchs, 7 from Plutarch, 5 from Philo, 1 from the Apostolic Fathers, 1 from the Greek Anthology, and 1 from Libanius. That makes it very difficult to accept anyone's claim that *head* in Greek could not mean "ruler" or "authority over."

The other interesting conclusion from this study is that no instances were discovered in which *kephalē* had the meaning "source, origin." This data stands in contradiction to the last sentence of the following key section in the Mickelsens' article:

> In classical Greek "head" usually meant a person's physical head; as a figure of speech it sometimes stood for the whole person or for life itself (e.g., "I stake my head on that"); or it could also mean the brim or upper part of something, as the "head" of an architectural column. A more common meaning was source, or origin, as we use it in the "head of the Mississippi river."[21]

In this last sentence "more common" apparently means more common than the other instances in which *kephalē* was used as a "figure of speech." But the Mickelsens give us no data

21. Mickelsen and Mickelsen, "Male Dominance," p. 23.

to support their statement that the meaning "source or origin" was a more common metaphorical meaning than the others they mention. The reader may wonder what the basis was upon which the Mickelsens asserted that "source or origin" was a "more common meaning." They are claiming that this sense was "more common" than the meanings "person," "life," or "upper part." In our summary the meanings "person" (119 times), "life" (14 times), and "upper part, top, end" (69 times) occurred a total of 202 times out of 2,336, or 67 percent of the 302 times in which *kephalē* was used metaphorically. For the Mickelsens' statement to be true, they would need to find more than 202 instances of the meaning "source" in a sample of 2,336 occurrences. It is fair to conclude that 0 out of 2,336 instances is not "more common"— in fact, it is not common at all—and that this crucial statement in their very influential article is simply false.

Someone might suggest at this point that our study of *kephalē* has not been exhaustive. Although we checked 2,336 instances, that leaves almost 10,000 more instances in the data banks of the TLG project in California. Perhaps those examples will show that *kephalē* can mean "source"?

To that suggestion I can only respond with an invitation to anyone who wishes to search for such evidence to go ahead and do so. Because the instances I checked represented a wide range of dates and types of literature, both religious (Jewish or Christian) and secular, it seems highly unlikely that additional significant senses will be found. Furthermore, it should be noted that my findings cover all the meanings mentioned in the major lexicons (although I have simplified the categories for the sake of presentation here).

Furthermore, any reader who wishes to search further in other literature must remember that in order for the evidence to be convincing for the time of the New Testament, it really ought to come from literature that is most representative of the Greek language at the time of the New Testament, namely, literature from the second or third century B.C. to the first century A.D. (I have conducted a much broader search simply to see if the meaning "source" might occur anywhere at all in Greek literature.) Moreover, the examples (if any are found) ought to be not simply cases that are so ambiguous that one can say they "might possibly" be understood to use *kephalē* as "source," but, in order to establish a clear case for that sense of the word, they ought to be cases in which the meaning is unambiguous and not easily explained in terms of other known senses of *kephalē*. (That is consistent with sound lexical research.) It seems safe to say that the likelihood of finding a sufficient number of unambiguous examples from texts near the time of the New Testament when none have been found by any scholars to date is, for all practical purposes, extremely low. If we are interested in biblical interpretation that is based on the facts of historical and linguistic research, then it would seem wise to give up once for all the claim that *kephalē* can mean "source."[22]

22. There are some other misstatements of fact in the article by the Mickelsens that should perhaps be noted at this point. Four times (twice on page 23 and twice on page 24) they give what they claim to be a "literal" translation of 1 Corinthians 11:3, where they tell the reader that they are giving "the actual words that Paul wrote" rather than a translator's interpretation. But in all four instances they insert the word *every* in the following phrase: "and head of *every* woman is the man." The effect of inserting the word *every* is to make more plausible their suggestion that the verse is referring to Adam (who was the "source" of Eve and, one might say, therefore of every woman). Furthermore, it makes the meaning "authority over," which they oppose, very difficult, for who wants to say that the authority over *every* woman is a man? But the word *every* should not be in this phrase: the Greek word for *every* (which here would be *pasēs*) is not in the Greek text, nor does the word *every* occur in any of the seven modern translations cited in their article.

    Another misstatement of fact occurs on page 26, where they attempt to show that the King James Version exhibits male chauvinism in Romans 16:1. There the KJV translates the word *diakonos* as "servant" to say that Phoebe is a "servant in the church at Cenchrea." The Mickelsens take exception to this translation, arguing that the word should be translated "deacon." They say "Only in reference to Phoebe does the King James translate Paul's word as 'servant.' In 1 Timothy 3:8, 12, it is translated 'deacon' but in all other places the King James uses the term 'minister.' Only of Phoebe is Paul's word *diakonos* translated 'servant.'"

    That gives the impression that the King James translators never used "servant" to translate *diakonos* except when their male bias intruded in dealing with Phoebe. But in fact, *diakonos* is translated by "servant" six

CITATIONS OF TEXTS IN WHICH *KEPHALĒ* MEANS "AUTHORITY OVER"

It remains now only to list those instances in which *kephalē* refers to a ruler or a person of superior authority or rank. These will be listed in largely chronological order.

---

other times in the KJV: Matthew 22:13 ("then said the king to the *servants*"); Matthew 23:11 ("the greatest among you shall be your *servant*"); Mark 9:35; John 2:5 ("his mother saith unto the *servants*"); John 2:9; and John 12:26 ("there shall also my *servant* be").

At the end of the article there is a short "Editor's Footnote," apparently not written by the Mickelsens but added by one of the editors of *Christianity Today*. The footnote claims that "The King James Version has twisted many a passage to save the male ego—or its chauvinistic theology" (page 29). Then three of the examples it cites contain errors themselves.

First, this editor claims, "The King James Version ... reverses the Greek order to place Aquila before Priscilla in deference to the husband—in spite of the fact that in the biblical text, Priscilla is clearly the leader (Acts 18:26)." Apparently the editor did not realize that the translators of the KJV used not our modern Greek New Testament but the Textus Receptus, which in fact has Aquila before Priscilla in this verse. They were not exhibiting male chauvinism but simply translating the Greek text as they had it.

Second, the editor says that in Psalm 68:11, the KJV misleadingly translates the verse to read "Great was the company of those that published the word of the Lord," whereas, the editor tells us, "The Hebrew is explicitly feminine: 'Great was the company of those women who published the word of the Lord.'" But this objection betrays a lack of knowledge of Hebrew grammar: terms that are grammatically "feminine" in Hebrew do not necessarily refer to feminine persons. That is especially true of collective nouns and titles and designations of office (many examples are listed in the Gesenius-Kautzsch-Cowley *Hebrew Grammar*, sections 122r,s). One familiar example is "the preacher" in Ecclesiastes 1:1: the Hebrew term *qoheleth* is grammatically "feminine" but it is used of "the son of David, king in Jerusalem" (Eccles. 1:1).

Third, the editor in the final point applauds the KJV because it "correctly notes the feminine Junia in Rom. 16:7 in contrast with most contemporary translations that with little or no justification transform ... the woman Junia into the man Junias to avoid the unthinkable—a woman among the apostles!" (page 29). But this assertion once again betrays a very superficial knowledge of Greek and wrongly attributes chauvinistic motives to those who come down on the side of a difficult exegetical question with which the editor disagrees. As a matter of fact, the name in Romans 16:7 could be either masculine or feminine (the accusative singular form would be exactly the same in this case). A. T. Robertson in his *Grammar of the Greek New Testament in the Light of Historical Research*

(1-2) In a statement in which the Delphic oracle warns the Argives to protect their full citizens from attack and thus the remainder of the population will be protected, it says, "Guarding your *head* from the blow; and the *head* shall shelter the body" (Herodotus 7.148.17).

(3) Although Plato does not use the word *kephalē* explicitly to refer to a *human* ruler or leader, he does say (in the text quoted earlier), that "the *head* ... is the most divine part and the one that reigns over all the parts within us" (*Timaeus* 44.D). This sentence does speak of the head as the ruling part of the body and therefore indicates that a metaphor that spoke of the leader or ruler of a group of people as its "head" would not have been unintelligible to Plato or his hearers.

The next instances come from the Septuagint.

(4) Judges 10:18: "And the people, the leaders of Gilead, said to one another, 'Who is the man that will begin to fight against the Ammonites? He shall be *head* over all the inhabitants of Gilead.'"[23]

(5) Judges 11:8: "And the elders of Gilead said to Jepthah, 'That is why we have turned to you now, that you may go with

---

(Nashville: Broadman, 1947, pp. 172-73) gives a long list of examples of personal names that had an abbreviated or shortened form at the time of the New Testament, thus indicating a very real possibility that Junias is a shortened form of the very common man's name Junianus, similar to the example of Silas/Silvanus.

What is most unfortunate about these misleading or erroneous factual statements is that they are made in a periodical that is widely read by Christians who have no technical ability to evaluate such arguments. Because they come from a reputable magazine and presumably from knowledgeable New Testament or Old Testament scholars, the ordinary readers have little choice but to accept them as true and therefore to mistrust their own English translations of the Bible wherever male-female relationships are discussed. Thus, the authority of God's Word in speaking to this area of life begins to be undercut—and needlessly so, for these claims that "male chauvinism" has distorted our translations are, in the instances cited, based on factual statements that are simply false.

23. This is the reading of the Alexandrinus text. Vaticanus has *archonta*, "ruler."

us and fight with the Ammonites, and be our *head* over all the inhabitants of Gilead.'"[24]

(6) Judges 11:9: "Jephtah said to the elders of Gilead, 'If you bring me home again to fight with the Ammonites, and the Lord gives them over to me, I will be your *head*.'"

(7) Judges 11:11: "So Jephthah went with the elders of Gilead, and all the people made him *head* and leader over them."

(8) 2 Kings (2 Samuel) 22:44: David says to God, "You shall keep me as the *head* of the Gentiles: a people which I knew not served me."

(9) 3 Kings (1 Kings) 8:1 (Alexandrinus): "Then Solomon assembled the elders of Israel and all the *heads* of the tribes."

(10) Psalm 17(18):43: David says to God, "You will make me *head* of the Gentiles: a people whom I knew not served me."

(11–12) Isaiah 7:8: "For the *head* of Syria is Damascus, and the *head* of Damascus is Rezin" (in both cases "head" means "ruler": Damascus is the city that rules over Syria, and Rezin is the king who rules over Damascus).

(13–14) Isaiah 7:9: "And the *head* of Ephraim is Samaria, and the *head* of Samaria is the son of Remaliah."

(15–16) Isaiah 9:14–16: (In the context of judgment) "So the Lord cut off from Israel *head* and tail ... the elder and honored man is the *head*, and the prophet who teaches lies is the tail; for those who lead this people lead them astray." Here the leaders of the people are called "head."

(17) Testament of Reuben 2:2: The seven spirits of deceit are the "*heads*" or "leaders" (*kephalai*, plural) of the works of innovation.

(18) Philo *On Dreams* 2.207: "'*Head*' we interpret allegorically to mean the ruling part of the soul."

(19) Philo *Moses* 2.30: "As the *head* is the ruling place in the living body, so Ptolemy became among kings."

(20) Philo *Moses* 2.82: "The mind is *head* and ruler of the sense-faculty in us."

---

24. In this verse and the next, the textual variant is the same as that mentioned in footnote 23.

(21–22) Philo *On Rewards and Punishments* 1.25: "The virtuous one, whether single man or people, will be the *head* of the human race and all the others will be like the parts of the body which are animated by the powers in the *head* and at the top."[25]

(The New Testament instances of *kephalē* will be treated at the end of this survey.)

(23) Plutarch *Pelopidas* 2.1.3: In an army, "the light-armed troops are like the hands, the cavalry like the feet, the line of men-at-arms itself like chest and breastplate, and the general is like the *head*."

(24–25) Plutarch *Cicero* 14.4: Catiline says to Cicero, criticizing the Senate as weak and the people as strong, "There are two bodies, one lean and wasted, but with a *head*, and the other headless but strong and large. What am I doing wrong if I myself become a *head* for this?" In saying this, Catiline was threatening to become the head of the people and thus to lead the people in revolt against Cicero. Therefore, "Cicero was all the more alarmed."[26]

(26) Plutarch *Galba* 4.3: "Vindex ... wrote to Galba inviting him to assume the imperial power, and thus to serve what was a vigorous body in need of a *head*."

(27) We may also mention here Plutarch *Agesilaus* 2.5, where a ruler who follows popular opinions is compared to a serpent whose tail insisted on leading the body instead of it being led by the *head*. The serpent consequently harmed itself. The implication is that a ruler should be like the "head" of a serpent and thereby lead the people.

(28–29) Plutarch *Table Talk* 7.7 (692.E.1): "We affectionately

25. There is a sense here of the members of the "body" being encouraged and directed by the virtuous leaders who are the "head," but there is no sense in which the ordinary people derive their being or existence from the leaders who are the "head"; thus, "source" would be an inappropriate sense of *kephalē* here as well.

26. These instances from Plutarch show that the sense "authority over" for *kephalē* was not merely a result of carrying over the force of the Hebrew term *ro'sh* into the Septuagint, for Plutarch was not influenced by the Hebrew Old Testament or the LXX in his use of words, nor were most of his readers.

call a person 'soul' or '*head*" from his ruling parts." Here the metaphor of the head ruling the body is clear, as is the fact that the head controls the body in *Table Talk* 3.1 (647.C): "For pure wine, when it attacks the *head* and severs the body from the control of the mind, distresses a man."

(30) Hermas *Similitudes* 7.3: The man is told that his family "cannot be punished in any other way than if you, the *head* of the house, be afflicted."

(31) Aquila, Deuteronomy 5:23: "The *heads* of tribes."

(32) Aquila, Deuteronomy 29:10(9): "The *heads* of tribes."

(33) Aquila, 3 Kings (1 Kings) 8:1: "Solomon assembled all the elders of Israel and all the *heads* of the tribes."

(34) Aquila, Ezekiel 38:2: Gog is called the "ruling *head* of Meshech."

(35) Theodotian, Judges 10:28: "He will be *head* over all the inhabitants of Gilead."

(36) Libanius *Oration* 20.3.15: People who derided government authorities are said to have "heaped on their own *heads* insults."

(37) *Greek Anthology* 8.19 (Epigram of Gregory of Nazianus, fourth century A.D,): Gregory is called the "*head* of a wife and three children."

With these examples as background, we can examine several New Testament texts in which *head* seems to take the well-established sense of "ruler" or "authority over."

(38–42) 1 Corinthians 11:3: "I want you to know that the *head* of every man is Christ, and the *head* of the woman is the man, and the *head* of Christ is God." (Paul then uses this sense of head once again in verse 4 and another time in verse 5 to refer to a man who "dishonors his *head*" and a woman "dishonors her *head*.") If *kephalē* means "authority over," then we have a sense that is both appropriate to the context (for head coverings in the first century were a sign of relation to authority, and it is therefore the question of appropriate authority relationships that leads to the question of head covering in this passage), and is consistent with the rest of Scripture. In the personal relationships between the eternal members of the Trinity, though they are equal in deity and in all their attributes, they are different in respect to authority: the Father directs and commands and sends, whereas the Son responds and obeys and comes into the world. In theological terms, there is ontological equality with economic subordination among the members of the Trinity. And that authority relationship whereby God the Father is the "authority over" God the Son is reflected in Christ's authority over every man and in the man's authority over the woman.

In an excellent discussion,[27] James Hurley, argues convincingly that the sense "source" is impossible in this passage: "There is no way to construct a satisfactory set of parallels if we take 'head' to mean 'source' in 1 Corinthians 11:3." He shows that however we try to construct the parallels in the sense "source" there is an impossible result: Eve was physically taken out of Adam but we cannot say that every man was physically taken out of Christ. On the other hand, Christ was the agent in the creation of every man, but we cannot say that God the Father created God the Son. But if we say that God the Father was the creator of the human nature of Christ, then must we say that Adam was the creator of the human nature of Eve? Or if we say that God the Father gives the economic distinction of sonship to the Son, then must we say that Adam gives a distinct personality to Eve, or a man to a woman generally? In short, there is no sense of "source" in which the passage can be interpreted consistently within itself and with the rest of Scripture. We conclude that "authority over" is the correct sense for *head* in 1 Corinthians 11:3.

(43) Ephesians 1:22: "He has put all things under his feet and has made him the *head* over all things for the church." Here God the Father made Christ the authority over all things for the sake of and the benefit of the church.

(44) Ephesians 4:15: "We are to grow up in every way into him who is the *head*, into Christ, from whom the whole body, joined and knit together by every joint with which it is supplied,

27. Hurley, pp. 166–67.

when each part is working properly, makes bodily growth and upbuilds itself in love." In this passage, the context again shows Christ's lordship over the church (compare verses 8, 10–12, which speak of Christ's ascension into heaven and his bestowing gifts on the church). Thus, we are to continually grow up into conformity with the one who is the sovereign Lord ruling over the church, and it is the rule and direction and guidance "from him" by which the whole body works properly, grows, and "upbuilds itself in love." Here again the guiding and ruling function of Christ as head over the church is shown to direct all its activities and make it work properly.

(45–46) Ephesians 5:22–24: "Wives, be subject to your husbands, as to the Lord. For the husband is the *head* of the wife as Christ is the *head* of the church, his body, and is himself its Savior. As the church is subject to Christ, so let wives also be subject in everything to their husbands." In this context, the idea of subjection to an authority that is implied by the word *hypotassō* is very appropriately emphasized by the image of Christ as the "authority over" the church and the husband as the "authority over" the wife. And as Paul does in every context where he mentions authority within marriage, he immediately goes on to emphasize that that authority, that headship, must be exercised in love, in gentleness, and with consideration for one's wife above one's self (vv. 25–30).

(47) Colossians 1:18: "He is the *head* of the body, the church." Here Paul, in emphasizing the great superiority of Christ, reminds his readers that Christ is the exalted authority over the church.

(48) Colossians 2:10: "And you have come to fullness of life in him, who is the *head* of all rule and authority." Here Paul emphasizes that Christ is the authority over not only the church, but over all rulers and authorities, over all powers in the universe.

(49) Colossians 2:18–19: "Let no one disqualify you, insisting on self-abasement and worship of angels, taking his stand on visions, puffed up without reason by his sensuous mind, and not holding fast to the *head*, from whom the whole body, nourished

and knit together through its joints and ligaments, grows with a growth that is from God." Here Paul encourages his readers not to abandon Christ in favor of serving angels. If they were to do so, they would be like members of a body abandoning the head of that body because, Paul affirms, Christ is the only true "head" of the church. But again the idea of allegiance to Christ instead of to angels makes the mention of Christ as "authority over" the church an appropriate one in this context. Especially when we realize that the image of head involves not just authority but leadership, direction, guidance, and control, then the following idea of the whole body being knit together and growing together is appropriate. Whether the idea of "nourishing" carries an image of food that is transported through the mouth (a part of the head) to the rest of the body is not made clear here. If "source" were a common meaning for *head* elsewhere it might convey some such nuance in this passage also. But in fact no Greek-speaking reader would have thought of the sense "source" when reading *kephalē*, and that certainly is not the primary image or the one that caused Paul to mention "head" in this section.

At the end of this survey someone might raise one final objection. Someone might agree that our survey is correct in demonstrating that the sense "source" never occurred in Greek literature outside the Bible, but this person might still argue that "source" seems to "make sense" or "fit the context well" in certain New Testament passages. Therefore (it might be argued), we can still take *kephalē* to mean "source" in certain New Testament passages where that meaning seems to fit the context.

In response to such an argument, it must be said that it assumes a situation that simply could not have occurred. It assumes that Paul, when writing Ephesians (for example) to a large number of Christians in several churches in Asia Minor, would use a common word in a sense never before known in the Greek-speaking world and expect his readers to understand it, even though he gave them no explicit explanation that he was using the word in a new way. Furthermore, it assumes that the readers would think about and reject all the known senses of *kephalē* that were familiar to them, even though at least one of those senses ("authority over") would fit the context, and that after rejecting all the known senses they would somehow guess at the new sense in which Paul wanted it to be understood. But this is in fact an impossible situation, one that simply could not occur in the ordinary process of written communication. Unless "source" can be shown to be a recognized meaning for *kephalē* in the Greek-speaking world, we are forced to conclude that Paul's readers would never have thought of that meaning instead of other recognized meanings in any New Testament context.

Given these instances of *kephalē* used to mean "ruler, authority over," we must conclude that its omission from the Liddell-Scott lexicon was an oversight that we hope will be corrected in the next edition. That would bring Liddell-Scott into agreement with all the standard Greek lexicons that specialize in the New Testament period.

We may wonder why the meaning "ruler, authority over" was not common in earlier Greek literature such as that from the fourth and fifth centuries B.C. (Most of our examples of the meaning "authority over" are from the second century B.C. to the first century A.D.) One explanation may be that the adjective *kephalaios* ("head-like" or "of the head") functioned with this meaning instead. Thus, "the head-like person" (*ho kephalios*) could mean "the head person" or "the chief person." The Liddell-Scott lexicon lists under *kephalios* the following meanings: "Metaphorical, of persons, *the head* or *chief.*" It then lists eight examples of this sense. Thus, because the adjective or the adjective used as a substantive could function with this meaning in an earlier period, there was perhaps no need for the noun *kephalē* to take a similar meaning. However, later in the development of the language, as our study demonstrates, the noun *kephalē* also came to take this sense. It certainly would have been readily understood, as the adjective *kephailos* demonstrates. (Note also the compound word *kephalourgos,* "foreman of works," Liddell-Scott.)

The survey of instances of *kephalē* used to mean "authority over" is complete. If we were to go beyond the time of the New Testament into the Patristic writings (only two of our extra-biblical quotations in the list above came from after the first century A.D.), we could greatly expand this list of examples. The use of *kephalē* to mean "authority over" is common in the early church Fathers.[28] But this survey is probably sufficient to demonstrate that "source, origin" is nowhere clearly attested as a legitimate meaning for *kephalē,* and that the meaning "ruler, authority over" has sufficient attestation to establish it clearly as a legitimate sense for *kephalē* in Greek literature at the time of the New Testament. Indeed, it was a well-established and recognizable meaning, and it is the meaning that best suits the New Testament texts that speak of the relationship between men and women by saying that the man is the "head" of a woman and the husband is the "head" of the wife.

28. See the examples in G. Lampe, *A Patristic Greek Lexicon* (Oxford: Oxford U., 1961), p. 749.

Appendix 2:
Office in the New Testament (and the Ministry of Women)

Author's note: The Reformed Ecumenical Synod counts in its membership some thirty churches from Africa, Asia, Europe, North America, South America, and the South Pacific. Member churches in the United States are the Associate Reformed Presbyterian Church, the Christian Reformed Church of North America, the Orthodox Presbyterian Church, and the Reformed Presbyterian Church of North America (Covenanter). The "basis" of the RES is the Scriptures, about which the Synod's constitution says, "In their entirety as well as in every part thereof, [they] are the infallible and ever-abiding Word of the living Triune God absolutely authoritative in all matters of creed and conduct." This paper was presented to the RES in 1972 by the Advisory Committee, and its recommendations were adopted in an amended form. It is here reprinted verbatim, except that the Scripture quotations have been changed from the American Standard Version *to the* New American Standard Bible, *and that a few paragraphs have been omitted from section B, "Analysis."*

A. MATERIALS

1. Report of Study Committee on "Office in the New Testament" (*Agenda, Reformed Ecumenical Synod: Australia 1972,* pp. 69–105).

2. Appendix or Minority Report of Study Committee (*Agenda,* pp. 134–35).

3. Contribution from J. Firet (*Agenda Supplement,* pp. 19–25).

4. Women and Ecclesiastical Offices, from Reformed Church of Argentina (*Agenda Supplement,* pp. 115–17).

5. Women and Office, from Christian Church of Sumba (*Agenda Supplement,* p. 18).

6. Ecclesiastical Office and Ordination, from Christian Reformed Church in the U.S.A. (*Agenda Supplement,* pp. 123, 127–28).

B. ANALYSIS

"The study committee sought to carry out its assignment but at the same time indicated that the mandate cannot possibly be carried out literally by a study committee."[1] On the background of an in-depth study of the concept and nature of office in the Holy Scripture, the study committee gave particular attention to "the nature and essence of ordination and/or installation" in correlation with the New Testament expression of that activity by "a laying on of hands,"[2] and to the biblical teaching on "The Ministry of Women."[3] The study committee answered affirmatively to the question of the church of Brazil, whether an elder, in charge of the worship service, may pronounce the benediction. It argued that there is a unity of Word and sacrament and that therefore an elder gifted and called to minister the Word of God may also minister the benediction.[4]

The Appendix (or Minority Report) differed from the committee report in emphasizing the relationship between "the seven" of Acts 6 and the deacons of 1 Timothy 3 and Philippians 1:1, in distinguishing the work of Philip and Stephen as evangelists (cf. Acts 21:8) from their work as "the seven," in considering

1. "Report of Study Committee on 'Office in the New Testament,'" in *Agenda, Reformed Ecumenical Synod: Australia* 1972, p. 69.
2. Ibid., pp. 84–87.
3. Ibid., pp. 98–105.
4. Ibid., p. 87.

the special function of the evangelist as continuing in the church today, and in maintaining that the laying on of hands is a uniform and normative practice in the New Testament for all offices and should be followed today. . . .

C. OBSERVATIONS

1. *Office.* The word *office* itself is not found in the New Testament, but the concept is found, for example, in the word *episkopē* (1 Tim. 3:1) which may be rendered "office of bishop." More particularly, the Apostle Paul lists what may be designated as special offices in the church as gifts of Christ to the church (Eph. 4:11) and includes them among a wider list of *gifts* (*charismata*) (1 Cor. 12:4ff.; cf. v. 28; less explicitly in Rom. 12:3–8). The diversities of gifts are also diversities of *services* (*diakonia*) (1 Cor. 12:4; cf. v. 28) so that the words *service/servants* (*diakonia/diakonos*) become key words not only for the general office of believer but more particularly for special offices (for *diakonia* see Acts 1:25; 6:4; 12:25; 20:24; 21:19; Rom. 11:13; 1 Cor. 12:5; 16:15; 2 Cor. 4:1; 5:18; 6:3; 11:8; Col. 4:17; 1 Tim. 1:12; for *diakonos* see 1 Cor. 3:5; 2 Cor. 6:4; 11:23; Eph. 3:7; 6:21; Col. 1:7, 23, 25; 4:7; 1 Thess. 3:2, 1 Tim. 4:6; all on the background of Jesus' teaching in Matt. 20:25–28; Mark 10:42–45).

This concept of office, *service/servants,* covers a broad spectrum from the ministry of Paul the Apostle to that of fellow-workers such as Apollos and Timothy, and finally the term *diakonos* becomes a virtual technical term for that special office which is singularly involved in service, that of the *deacon* (1 Tim. 3:8–13; Phil. 1:1).

2. *Bishops (elders) and deacons.* In the midst of a variety of terminology in reference to special gifts, offices, and services, a pattern does emerge of designating two distinct special offices, those who rule and teach, and those who give aid and serve, or bishops and deacons (Phil. 1:1; 1 Tim. 3:1–13; cf. the latter with Acts 20:17 and 28, and Eph. 4:11). The distinction between these two offices is indicated by the qualifications and tasks required of each. The bishops (elders) are to rule and to teach (1 Tim.

3:2, 5; 5:17; Titus 1:9ff.; Acts 20:28 and chapter 15; 1 Peter 5:1–4), the deacons are to serve (cf. Acts 6:2–3). This distinction is also manifest in their distinctive names, *bishops*, (*episkopos*, those who oversee others) and *deacons* (*diakonos*, those who serve others).

3. *Elders* (bishops). Certain significant truths appear when Scripture is compared with Scripture: (a) The rule or oversight is conducted by a plurality of elders in their corporate capacity and on a parity with one another. The reference to this office in terms of its existence in a church and its activity of ruling is always made in the plural (Acts 11:30; 14:23; chapter 15; 20:17, 28; Phil. 1:1, 1 Tim. 5:17; Titus 1:5; see also the Scripture under the following section [b]). (b) When it is taken into account that elders may be referred to by two titles (presbyters or bishops, Acts 20:17, 28; Titus 1:5, 7) or may be designated by their activity of ruling and teaching without any title, and when it is recognized therefore that this rule by elders is evident in virtually every area of the New Testament church and is referred to by virtually every New Testament author (Acts 11:30; 14:23; chapter 15; 20:17, 28; Phil. 1:1; 1 Thess. 5:12–13; 1 Tim. 3:1ff.; 5:17; Titus 1:5; Heb. 13:7, 17; James 5:14; 1 Peter 5:1ff.; cf. Rom. 12:7–8; 1 Cor. 12:28; 16:15; 2 John 1; 3 John 1) as well as being commanded by Paul (Titus 1:5), it becomes apparent that the government by elders is the one and normative pattern in the New Testament. (c) Within the unity of the one office of elder there are some "who work hard at preaching and teaching (1 Tim. 5:17). This has given rise to the designations "teaching elder" or "minister," and "ruling elder" or simply "elder."

4. *Laying on of hands* (ordination and/or installation). The advisory committee notes that elders (1 Tim. 5:22) and "the seven" (Acts 6:6) as well as those commissioned for special service (Acts 13:3) were appointed or set apart by the laying on of hands of all those who are included under the designation "presbytery" (*presbyterion*, 1 Tim. 4:14; cf. 2 Tim. 1:6; Acts 6:6; 13:3). The present difference in practice indicates that the various churches of the RES should study this question again and communicate

their understanding of the New Testament practice and its significance.

5. *Ministry of women.* In view of the fact that the historic Christian and Reformed practice of limiting the office of ruling and preaching elders to men has been questioned by some churches in the RES[5] and that special attention has been given to this matter by the study committee report, the advisory committee would also give special attention to this in their observations so that it may be demonstrated "that it is the plain and obvious teaching of Scripture that women are excluded from the office of ruling and preaching elders." Two passages in the New Testament deal explicitly and directly with this subject in the context of the life of the church, 1 Timothy 2:11–15 and 1 Corinthians 14:33*b*–37. The Apostle, with his apostolic and thus normative authority, says specifically, "I do not allow a woman to teach or exercise authority over a man, but to remain quiet" (1 Tim. 2:12). The prohibition is motivated within the statement itself by the fact that a woman must be in subjection to man (v. 11) and teaching and ruling or dominion over a man is a violation of this subjection. The reason for this prohibition is given in verses 13 and 14: "For it was Adam who was first created, and then Eve. And it was not Adam who was deceived, but the woman being quite deceived, fell into transgression." It may be summarized as the priority of Adam's (man's) creation to that of Eve (woman) and the fact of Eve's (woman's) being deceived or led astray. Paul thus appeals to the two great facts of God's significant order in creating man and woman and to the implications of the fall. The reference to the priority of Adam's creation to that of Eve refers to Genesis 2:18–25 with its teaching that the woman is created to assist man and be in subjection to him as the one who is the head over her (cf. 1 Cor. 11:2ff. and Eph. 5:22ff.). The significance of Eve's deception as a reason for the prohibition is not indicated here or elsewhere in the Scriptures. In the 1 Corinthians 14:33*b*–37 passage a similar prohibi-

5. *Acts of Reformed Ecumenical Synod: Amsterdam 1968,* art. 84, p. 39, and items 3–5 of the materials.

tion is given, and there also reasons are given. The reasons are that women are to be in subjection "as the Law also says" (v. 34) and that "it is improper for a woman to speak in church" (v. 35). Here the Apostle indicates that God's law demands such subjection of women that they do not speak and teach in the church and that a violation of that demand of God's law is in itself shameful. Apparently the Corinthian church thought and practiced otherwise than Paul taught and apparently they had argued for a supposedly more liberated view of woman in the church (v. 36). Paul indicates that the command that women keep silence in the churches is to be observed in their church "as in all the churches of the saints" (v. 33*b*). Further, he rebukes their practice of letting women speak and teach contrary to the law of God and the practice in all the churches by asking in effect if only they have the word of God (v. 36). Finally, he concludes by indicating that this teaching about women not speaking and teaching in church is to be acknowledged by them and recognized as one of the things that "are the Lord's commandment" (v. 37). It should be carefully noted that these passages (1 Tim. 2:11–15; 1 Cor. 14:33*b*–37) are not illustrations but commands, and that the reasons or grounds given are not time-bound, historically and culturally relative arguments that grow up out of or apply only to that day and age, but rather the way God created man and woman and the relationships God commanded that they should sustain to one another. When we realize that the office of ruling and preaching elders has as its essence the responsibility to teach in the church and to rule or have dominion in that church (see above), and that in reference to men also, we see that these commands of Paul exclude women from this office.

The fact that "there is neither male nor female, for you are all one in Christ Jesus" (Gal. 3:28) does not deny the teaching of 1 Timothy 2 and 1 Corinthians 14 just as it does not deny man's maleness and woman's femaleness nor annul their relationship in the family (cf. Eph. 5:22ff.; for the significance of the correlation of man's rule in the family with his rule in the church, see 1 Timothy 3:4–5).

Even though 1 Timothy 2:11–15 and 1 Corinthians 14:33*b*– 37 exclude women from the teaching and ruling office in the church, other passages indicate that women are involved in diaconal tasks and even in appropriate teaching situations. A sampling of these activities may be seen in the following: older widows are enrolled by the church (1 Tim. 5:9–16); older women are called upon to teach and train young women in reference to their responsibilities to their husbands and children (Titus 2:3– 4); women (or wives, *gunaikas*) are referred to in the midst of the description of deacons (1 Tim. 3:11); Phoebe is designated as "a servant [*diakonon*] of the church which is at Cenchrea" (Rom. 16:1); Paul referred to a situation in the Corinthian church where women are praying or prophesying (1 Cor. 11:5); and Priscilla and Aquila, that inseparable wife-and-husband team, in a discreet and private meeting, expounded unto Apollos "the way of God more accurately" (Acts 18:26).

In considering the ministry of women in the church these three biblical truths must be held in correlation: (1) "There is neither male nor female; for you are all one in Christ Jesus" (Gal. 3:28); in their standing in and before Christ male and female are equal. (2) Women, by God's creative order, are to be in subjection to men in the home and church, and are therefore excluded from the office of ruling and preaching elders (Eph. 5:22; 1 Tim. 2:11–15; 1 Cor. 14:33*b*–37; 1 Tim. 3:4–5). (3) Women have a unique function to fulfill in the diaconal task of the church and in appropriate teaching situations (cf., for example, 1 Tim. 3:11; 5:9ff.; Titus 2:3–4; Rom. 16:1).

D. RECOMMENDATIONS:

1. That Synod request the member churches to study further the biblical teaching concerning "the laying on of hands" (ordination and/or installation) and present their finding to the next Synod of the RES. *Ground:* There is divergence of understanding and practice among the churches and such re-evaluation of the Scriptures may hopefully bring the churches to a unified understanding and practice.

2. That Synod call the attention of the Reformed Church in Brazil to the argument and affirmative answer provided by the study committee to their question. *Ground:* The Reformed Church in Brazil has asked the RES for its advice and this is the answer the study committee has provided from their consideration of the Scriptures.

3. That Synod reaffirm that it is the teaching of Scripture that women are excluded from the office of ruling and preaching elders. *Ground:* The Scriptures indicate that for all the churches women are not permitted to teach nor to have dominion over men on the basis of God's order of creation, the implication of the fall, the explicit statement of the law, and the fact that the Apostle's command is itself "the commandment of the Lord" (1 Tim. 2:11–15; 1 Cor. 14:33b–37).

4. That the Synod recommend to the member churches that because there is no clear Scriptural evidence for women occupying the office of deacons, they make full use of the gifts and services of women in the diaconal task in an auxiliary capacity and in appropriate teaching situations. *Ground:* Compare 1 Timothy 3:8–13 and the verses referred to above indicating the diaconal tasks and appropriate teaching situation of women.

GEORGE W. KNIGHT III
Reporter

Index of Subjects

Index of Persons

Index of Scripture

Moody Press, a ministry of the Moody Bible Institute, is designed for education, evangelization, and edification. If we may assist you in knowing more about Christ and the Christian life, please write us without obligation: Moody Press, c/o MLM, Chicago, IL 60610.